Date Due

DE 13 '68	DE 1 '95		
JA 10 69			
FE 27 70			
JUN 12 1970			
DE 21 74			
NV 29 77			
JE 6 80			
DE 8 80			

PS3554
I32A6
1967

RIVERSIDE CITY COLLEGE
LIBRARY
Riverside, California

PRINTED IN U.S.A.

James Dickey POEMS 1957-1967

James
Dickey

POEMS 1957-1967

WESLEYAN UNIVERSITY PRESS

Middletown, Connecticut

Riverside Community College
Library
4800 Magnolia Avenue
Riverside, CA 92506

Copyright © 1958, 1959, 1960, 1961, 1962, 1963, 1964,
1965, 1966, 1967 by James Dickey

Library of Congress Catalog Card Number: 67–15230
Manufactured in the United States of America
First printing April, 1967; second printing June, 1967

To Maxine, my wife

Contents

Helmets

Buckdancer's Choice

Falling

Acknowledgments

MANY of these poems first appeared in publications other than volumes by the author. For their courtesy in granting permission to reprint and in assigning copyrights, grateful acknowledgment is made to the editors of the following: *Atlantic Monthly, Beloit Poetry Journal, The Bulletin* (Sydney, Australia), *Choice, Commentary, Encounter, Harper's Magazine, Hudson Review, Kenyon Review, The Nation, The New Yorker, North American Review, Paris Review, Partisan Review, Poetry, Poetry Dial, Quarterly Review of Literature, Saturday Evening Post, Saturday Review, Sewanee Review, Shenandoah, Southern Review, Transatlantic Review, Virginia Quarterly Review,* and *Yale Review.*

Among poems originally printed in *Poetry* are these: "The Being," "A Dog Sleeping on my Feet," "Dover: Believing in Kings," "The Firebombing," "A Folk Singer of the Thirties," "The Hospital Window," "Inside the River," and Part II of "On the Coosawattee."

Poems that first appeared in *The New Yorker* include the following: "Angina," "At Darien Bridge," "The Aura," "A Birth," "Buckdancer's Choice," "Bums, on Waking," "Cherrylog Road," "Coming Back to America," "The Common Grave," "The Driver," "The Dusk of Horses," "Encounter in the Cage Country," "The Escape," "Falling," "False Youth: Two Seasons (II)," "Fence Wire," "For the Nightly Ascent of the Hunter Orion over a Forest Clearing," "Goodbye to Serpents," "The Heaven of Animals," "Hedge Life," "The Ice Skin," "In the Marble Quarry," "In the Mountain Tent," "In the Tree House at Night," "Kudzu," "The Lifeguard," "Listening to Foxhounds," "The Magus," "The Movement of Fish," "The Poisoned Man," "Power and Light," "Reincarnation (I)," "The Salt Marsh," "The Scarred Girl," "The Shark's Parlor," "Snakebite," "Sun," "Them, Crying," "Trees and Cattle," "The Underground Stream," "Walking on Water," "The War Wound," Part I of "On the Coosawattee," and a slightly shorter version of "Slave Quarters."

Sermon

MAY DAY SERMON TO THE WOMEN
OF GILMER COUNTY, GEORGIA,
BY A WOMAN PREACHER LEAVING THE BAPTIST CHURCH

Each year at this time I shall be telling you of the Lord
—Fog, gamecock, snake and neighbor—giving men all the help they
    need
To drag their daughters into barns. Children, I shall be showing you
The fox hide stretched on the door   like a flying squirrel   fly
Open   to show you the dark where the one pole of light is paid out
In spring by the loft, and in it the croker sacks sprawling and shuttling
Themselves into place as it comes   comes   through spiders dead
Drunk on their threads   the hogs' fat bristling   the milk
Snake in the rafters unbending through gnats to touch the last place
Alive on the sun with his tongue   I shall be flickering from my mouth
Oil   grease cans   lard cans   nubbins   cobs   night
Coming   floating   each May with night coming I cannot help
Telling you how he hauls her to the centerpole   how the tractor moves
Over as he sets his feet and hauls   hauls   ravels her arms and hair
In stump chains: Telling: telling of Jehovah come and gone
Down on His belly   descending   creek-curving   blowing His legs

Like candles, out   putting North Georgia copper on His head
To crawl in under the door in dust red enough to breathe
The breath of Adam into: Children, be brought where she screams
    and begs
To the sacks of corn and coal   to nails   to the swelling ticks
On the near side of mules, for the Lord's own man has found the limp
Rubber that lies in the gulley   the penis-skin like a serpent
Under the weaving willow.
                    Listen: often a girl in the country,
Mostly sweating   mostly in spring, deep enough in the holy Bible
Belt, will feel her hair rise up   arms rise, and this not any wish

Of hers, and clothes like lint shredding off her   abominations
In the sight of the Lord: will hear the Book speak like a father
Gone mad: each year at this time will hear the utmost sound
Of herself, as her lungs cut, one after one, every long track
Spiders have coaxed from their guts   stunned spiders fall
Into Pandemonium   fall   fall   and begin to dance like a girl

On the red clay floor of Hell   she screaming   her father screaming
Scripture   CHAPter and verse   beating it into her with a weeping
Willow branch   the animals stomping   she prancing and climbing
Her hair   beasts shifting from foot to foot about the stormed
Steel of the anvil   the tractor gaslessly straining   believing
It must pull up a stump   pull   pull down the walls of the barn
Like Dagon's temple   set the Ark of the Lord in its place   change all
Things for good, by pain. Each year at this time you will be looking up
Gnats in the air   they boil   recombine   go mad with striving
To form the face of her lover, as when he lay at Nickajack Creek
With her by his motorcycle   looming   face trembling with exhaust
Fumes   humming insanely—each May you hear her father scream
    like God
And King James as he flails   cuds richen   bulls chew themselves
    whitefaced
Deeper into their feed bags, and he cries something the Lord   cries
Words! Words! Ah, when they leap   when they are let out of the
    Bible's
Black box   they whistle   they grab the nearest girl and do her hair up
For her lover in root-breaking chains   and she knows she was born
    to hang
In the middle of Gilmer County   to dance, on May Day, with holy
Words all around her   with beasts with insects   O children NOW
In five bags of chicken-feed the torsoes of prophets form   writhe
Die out as her freckled flesh   as flesh and the Devil twist and turn
Her body to love   cram her mouth with defiance   give her words
To battle with the Bible's in the air: she shrieks sweet Jesus and God
I'm glad   O my God-darling   O lover   O angel-stud   dear heart
Of life put it in me   *give*   you're killing   KILLING: each
Night each year at this time I shall be telling you of the snake-
doctor drifting from the loft, a dragon-fly, where she is wringing
Out the tractor's muddy chains   where her cotton socks prance,
Where her shoes as though one ankle were broken, stand with night
Coming   and creatures drawn by the stars, out of their high holes
By moon-hunger driven   part the leaves   crawl out of Grimes Nose
And Brasstown Bald: on this night only I can tell how the weasel pauses
Each year in the middle of the road   looks up at the evening blue
Star   to hear her say again   O again   YOU CAN BEAT ME
    TO DEATH
And I'll still be glad:

Sisters, it is time to show you rust
Smashing the lard cans more in   spring after spring   bullbats
Swifts   barn swallows   mule bits clashing on walls   mist turning
Up white out of warm creeks: all over, fog taking the soul from the body
Of water   gaining   rising up trees   sifting up through smoking green
Frenzied levels of gamecocks sleeping from the roots   stream-curves
Of mist: wherever on God's land is water, roads rise up the shape of
    rivers
Of no return: O sisters, it is time   you cannot sleep with Jehovah

Searching for what to be, on ground that has called Him from His Book:
Shall He be the pain in the willow, or the copperhead's kingly riding
In kudzu, growing with vines toward the cows   or the wild face
    working over
A virgin, swarming like gnats   or the grass of the west field, bending
East, to sweep into bags and turn brown   or shall He rise, white on
    white,
From Nickajack Creek as a road?   The barn creaks like an Ark   beasts
Smell everywhere the streams drawn out by their souls   the flood-
sigh of grass in the spring   they shall be saved   they know as she
    screams
Of sin   as the weasel stares   the hog strains toward the woods
That hold its primeval powers:
                                    Often a girl in the country will find
    herself
Dancing with God in a mule's eye, twilight drifting in straws from the
    dark
Overhead of hay   cows working their sprained jaws sideways at the
    hour
Of night all things are called: when gnats in their own midst and fury
Of swarming-time, crowd into the barn   their sixty-year day consumed
In this sunset   die in a great face of light that swarms and screams
Of love.
            Each May you will crouch like a sawhorse to make yourself
More here   you will be cow chips   chickens croaking for her hands
That shook the corn over the ground   bouncing   kicked this way
And that, by the many beaks   and every last one of you will groan
Like nails barely holding   and your hair be full of the gray
Glints of stump chains.   Children, each year at this time you will have
Back-pain, but also heaven   but also   also this lovely other life-

Sermon   5

pain between the thighs: woman-child or woman in bed in Gilmer
County   smiling in sleep like blood-beast and Venus together
Dancing the road as I speak, get up   up in your socks and take
The pain you were born for: that rose through her body straight
Up from the earth like a plant, like the process that raised overhead
The limbs of the uninjured willow.

                         Children, it is true
That the kudzu advances, its copperheads drunk and tremendous
With hiding, toward the cows   and wild fences cannot hold the string
Beans as they overshoot their fields: that in May the weasel loves love
As much as blood   that in the dusk bottoms young deer stand half
In existence, munching cornshucks   true that when the wind blows
Right   Nickajack releases its mist   the willow-leaves stiffen once
More   altogether   you can hear   each year at this time you can hear
No   Now, no   Now   Yes   Again   More   O   O my God
I love it   love you   don't leave   don't   don't stop O GLORY
Be:

        More dark   more coming   fox-fire crawls over the okra-
patch   as through it a real fox creeps to claim his father's fur
Flying on doornails   the quartermoon on the outhouse begins to shine
With the quartermoonlight of this night   as she falls and rises,
Chained to a sapling like a tractor   WHIPPED for the wind in the
    willow
Tree   WHIPPED for Bathsheba and David   WHIPPED for the
    woman taken
Anywhere   anytime   WHIPPED for the virgin sighing   bleeding
From her body   for the sap and green of the year   for her own good
And evil:

           Sisters, who is your lover? Has he done nothing but come
And go?   Has your father nailed his cast skin to the wall as evidence
Of sin?   Is it flying like a serpent in the darkness   dripping pure
    radiant venom
Of manhood?

           Yes, but *he* is unreeling in hills between his long legs
The concrete of the highway   his face in the moon beginning
To burn   twitch   dance like an overhead swarm   he feels a nail
Beat through his loins far away   he rises in pain and delight, as spirit
Enters his sex   sways   forms   rises with the forced, choked, red
Blood of her red-headed image, in the red-dust, Adam-colored clay
Whirling and leaping   creating   calling: O on the dim, gray man-

6

track of cement flowing into his mouth   each year he turns the moon
    back
Around on his handlebars   her image going all over him like the wind
Blasting up his sleeves. He turns off the highway, and
                                                    Ah, children,
There is now something élse to hear: there is now this madness of
    engine
Noise in the bushes   past reason   ungodly   squealing   reverting
Like a hog turned loose in the woods   Yes, as he passes the first
Trees of God's land   gamehens overhead   and the farm is ON
Him   everything is more   *more*   MORE as he enters the black
Bible's white swirling ground   O daughters   his heartbeat great
With trees   some blue leaves coming   NOW   and right away fire
In the right eye   Lord   more   MORE   O Glory   land
Of Glory: ground-branches hard to get through   coops where
    fryers huddle
To death, as the star-beast dances and scratches at their home-boards,
His rubber stiffens on its nails: Sisters, understand about men and
    sheaths:

About nakedness: understand how butterflies, amazed, pass out
Of their natal silks   how the tight snake takes a great breath   bursts
Through himself and leaves himself behind   how a man casts finally
Off everything that shields him from another   beholds his loins
Shine with his children forever   burn with the very juice
Of resurrection: such shining is how the spring creek comes
Forth from its sunken rocks   it is how the trout foams and turns on
Himself   heads upstream, breathing mist like water, for the cold
Mountain of his birth   flowing   sliding in and through the ego-
maniacal sleep of gamecocks   shooting past a man with one new blind
Side   who feels his skinned penis rise like a fish through the dark
Woods, in a strange lifted-loving form   a snake about to burst
Through itself on May Day   and leave behind on the ground   still
Still   the shape of a fooled thing's body:
                                            he comes on   comes
Through the laurel, wiped out on his right by an eye-twig   now he
Is crossing the cowtrack   his hat in his hand going on before
His face   then up   slowly over   over like the Carolina moon
Coming into Georgia   feels the farm close its Bible and ground-
fog over him   his dark side blazing   something whipping

By, beyond sight: each year at this time I shall be letting you
Know when she cannot stand   when the chains fall back on
To the tractor   when you should get up   when neither she nor the
     pole
Has any more sap   and her striped arms and red hair must keep her
From falling   when she feels God's willow laid on her, at last,
With no more pressure than hay, and she has finished crying to her
     lover's
Shifting face   and his hand when he gave it   placed it, unconsumed,
In her young burning bush.   Each year by dark she has learned

That home is to hang in   home is where your father cuts the baby
Fat from your flanks for the Lord, as you scream for the viny foreskin
Of the motorcycle rider. Children, by dark   by now, when he drops
The dying branch and lets her down   when the red clay flats
Of her feet hit the earth   all things have heard—fog, gamecock
Snake and lover—and we listen: Listen, children, for the fog to lift
The form of sluggish creeks into the air: each spring, each creek
On the Lord's land flows in two   O sisters, lovers, flows in two
Places: where it was, and in the low branches of pines where chickens
Sleep in mist   and that is where you will find roads floating free
Of the earth   winding   leading unbrokenly out of the farm of God
The father:
               Each year at this time she is coming from the barn   she
Falls once, hair hurting her back   stumbles walking naked
With dignity   walks with no help to the house   lies face down
In her room, burning   tuning in   hearing in the spun rust-
groan of bedsprings, his engine root and thunder like a pig,
Knowing who it is   must be   knowing that the face of gnats will wake
In the woods, as a man: there is nothing else this time of night
But her dream of having wheels between her legs: tires, man,
Everything she can hold, pulsing together   her father walking
Reading   intoning   calling   his legs blown out by the ground-
fogging creeks of his land: Listen   listen like females each year
In May   O glory   to the sound   the sound of your man gone wild
With love in the woods   let your nipples rise   and leave your feet
To hear: This is when moths flutter in from the open, and Hell
Fire of the oil lamp shrivels them   and it is said
To her: said like the Lord's voice trying to find a way
Outside the Bible   O sisters   O women and children who will be

Women of Gilmer County   you farm girls and Ellijay cotton mill
Girls, get up   each May Day   up in your socks   it is the father
Sound   going on about God   making, a hundred feet down,
The well beat its bucket like a gong: she goes to the kitchen,
Stands with the inside grain of pinewood whirling on her like a cloud
Of wire   picks up a useful object   two   they are not themselves
Tonight   each hones itself as the moon does   new by phases
Of fog   floating unchanged into the house   coming atom
By atom   sheepswool   different smokes   breathed like the Word
Of nothing, round her seated father. Often a girl in the country,
Mostly in spring   mostly bleeding   deep enough in the holy Bible
Belt   will feel her arms rise up   up   and this not any wish
Of hers   will stand, waiting for word.   O daughters, he is rambling
In Obadiah   the pride of thine heart hath deceived thee, thou
That dwelleth in the clefts of the rock, whose habitation is high
That saith in his heart   O daughters   who shall bring me down
To the ground?   And she comes down   putting her back into
The hatchet   often   often   he is brought down   laid out
Lashing   smoking   sucking wind: Children, each year at this time
A girl will tend to take an ice pick in both hands   a lone pine
Needle   will hover   hover: Children, each year at this time
Things happen quickly   and it is easy for a needle to pass
Through the eye of a man bound for Heaven   she leaves it   naked goes
Without further sin through the house   floating in and out of all
Four rooms   comes onto the porch on cloud-feet   steps down and out
And around to the barn   pain changing   her old screams hanging
By the hair around her: Children, in May, often a girl in the country
Will find herself lifting wood   her arms like hair rising up
To undo locks   raise latches   set gates aside   turn all things
Loose   shoo them out   shove   kick   and hogs are leaping ten
Million years back through fog   cows walking worriedly passing out
Of the Ark   from stalls where God's voice cursed and mumbled
At milking time   moving   moving   disappearing   drifting
In cloud   cows in the alders already lowing far off   no one
Can find them each year: she comes back to the house and grabs double
Handfuls of clothes
                    and her lover, with his one eye of amazing grace
Of sight, sees her coming as she was born   swirling   developing
Toward him   she hears him grunt   she hears him creaking

His saddle   dead-engined   she conjures one foot whole from the
    ground-
fog to climb him behind   he stands up   stomps   catches   roars
Blasts the leaves from a blinding twig   wheels   they blaze up
Together   she breathing to match him   her hands on his warm belly
His hard blood renewing like a snake   O now   now as he twists
His wrist, and takes off with their bodies:
                                                    each May you will hear it
Said that the sun came as always   the sun of next day burned
Them off with the mist: that when the river fell back on its bed
Of water   they fell from life   from limbs   they went with it
To Hell   three-eyed   in love, their legs around an engine, her arms
Around him.   But now, except for each year at this time, their sound
Has died: except when the creek-bed thicks its mist   gives up
The white of its flow to the air   comes off   lifts into the pinepoles
Of May Day   comes back as you come awake in your socks and
    crotchhair
On new-mooned nights of spring   I speak   you listen and the pines
    fill
With motorcycle sound as they rise, stoned out of their minds on the
    white
Lightning of fog   singing   the saddlebags full of her clothes
Flying   snagging   shoes hurling away   stockings grabbed-off
Unwinding and furling on twigs: all we know   all we could follow
Them by was her underwear   was stocking after stocking where it tore
Away, and a long slip stretched on a thorn   all these few gave
Out. Children, you know it: that place was where they took
Off into the air   died   disappeared   entered my mouth   your mind
Each year   each pale, curved breath   each year as she holds him
Closer wherever he hurtles   taking her   taking her   she going
    forever
Where he goes   with the highways of rivers   through one-eyed
Twigs   through clouds of chickens   and grass with them bends
Double   the animals lift their heads   peanuts and beans exchange
Shells in joy   joy like the speed of the body and rock-bottom
Joy: joy by which the creek bed appeared to bear them out of the Bible
's farm   through pine-clouds of gamecocks where no earthly track
Is, but those risen out of warm currents   streams born to hang
In the pines of Nickajack Creek: tonight her hands are under
His crackling jacket   the pain in her back enough to go through

Them both   her buttocks blazing in the sheepskin saddle: tell those
Who look for them   who follow by rayon stockings   who look on human
Highways   on tracks of cement and gravel   black weeping roads
Of tar: tell them that she and her rider have taken no dirt
Nor any paved road   no path for cattle   no county trunk or trail
Or any track upon earth, but have roared like a hog on May Day
Through pines and willows: that when he met the insane vine
Of the scuppernong   he tilted his handlebars back and took
The road that rises in the cold mountain spring from warm creeks:
O women in your rayon from Lindale, I shall be telling you to go
To Hell   by cloud   down where the chicken walk is running
To weeds   and anyone can show you where the tire marks gave out
And her last stocking was cast   and you stand as still as a weasel
Under Venus   before you dance   dance yourself blue with blood-
joy looking into the limbs   looking up into where they rode
Through cocks tightening roots with their sleep-claws. Children,
They are gone: gone as the owl rises, when God takes the stone
Blind sun off its eyes, and it sees   sees hurtle in the utter dark
Gold of its sight, a boy and a girl buried deep in the cloud
Of their speed   drunk, children   drunk with pain and the throttle
Wide open, in love   with a mindless sound   with her red hair
In the wind streaming gladly for them both   more than gladly
As the barn settles under the weight of its pain   the stalls fill once
More with trampling like Exodus   the snake doctor gone the rats beginning
On the last beans   and all the chicks she fed, each year at this time
Burst from their eggs as she passes:
                              Children, it is true that mice
No longer bunch on the rafters, but wade the fields like the moon,
Shifting in patches   ravenous   the horse floats, smoking with flies,
To the water-trough   coming back less often   learning to make
Do with the flowing drink of deer   the mountain standing   cold
Flowing into his mouth   grass underfoot   dew   horse or what
ever he is now   moves back into trees where the bull walks
With a male light spread between his horns   some say screams like
    a girl
And her father yelling together:
                              Ah, this night in the dark laurel
Green of the quartermoon I shall be telling you that the creek's last

Sermon   11

Ascension is the same   is made of water and air   heat and cold
This year as before: telling you not to believe every scream you hear
Is the Bible's: it may be you or me   it may be her sinful barn-
howling for the serpent, as her father whips her, using the tried
And true rhythms of the Lord.   Sisters, an old man at times like this
Moon, is always being found   yes found with an ice-pick on his mind,
A willow limb in his hand.   By now, the night-moths have come
Have taken his Bible and read it   have flown, dissolved, having found
Nothing in it for them.   I shall be telling you at each moon   each
Year at this time, Venus rises   the weasel goes mad at the death
In the egg, of the chicks she fed for him by hand: mad in the middle
Of human space he dances   blue-eyed   dances with Venus rising
Like blood-lust over the road   O tell your daughters   tell them
That the creek's ghost can still   O still can carry double
Weight of true lovers   any time   any night as the wild turkeys claw
Into the old pines of gamecocks   and with a cow's tongue, the Bible
    calls
For its own, and is not heard   and even God's unsettled great
    white father-
head with its ear to the ground, cannot hear   know   cannot pick
Up where they are   where her red hair is streaming through the white
Hairs of His centerless breast: with the moon   He cries with the
    cow all
Its life penned up with Noah in the barn   talk of original
Sin as the milk spurts   talk of women   talk of judgment and flood
And the promised land:
                    Telling on May Day, children: telling
That the animals are saved without rain   that they are long gone
From here   gone with the sun   gone with the woman taken
In speed   gone with the one-eyed mechanic   that the barn falls in
Like Jericho at the bull's voice   at the weasel's dance   at the hog's
Primeval squeal   the uncut hay walks when the wind prophesies in
    the west
Pasture   the animals move, with kudzu creating all the earth
East of the hayfield: Listen: each year at this time the county speaks
With its beasts and sinners   with its blood: the county speaks of
    nothing
Else each year at this time: speaks as beasts speak to themselves
Of holiness learned in the barn: Listen   O daughters   turn   turn
In your sleep   rise with your backs on fire   in spring   in your socks

12

Into the arms of your lovers: every last one of you, listen one-eyed
With your man   in hiding   in fog where the animals walk through
The white breast of the Lord   muttering   walk with nothing
To do but be   in the spring laurel in the mist and self-sharpened
Moon   walk through the resurrected creeks   through the Lord
At their own pace   the cow shuts its mouth and the Bible is still
Still open at anything   we are gone   the barn wanders over the earth.

Into the Stone

All dark is now no more.
This forest is drawing a light.
All Presences change into trees.
One eye opens slowly without me.
My sight is the same as the sun's,
For this is the grave of the king,
Where the earth turns, waking a choir.
     All dark is now no more.

Birds speak, their voices beyond them.
A light has told them their song.
My animal eyes become human
As the Word rises out of the darkness
Where my right hand, buried beneath me,
Hoveringly tingles, with grasping
The source of all song at the root.
     Birds sing, their voices beyond them.

     Put down those seeds in your hand.
These trees have not yet been planted.
A light should come round the world,
Yet my army blanket is dark,
That shall sparkle with dew in the sun.
My magical shepherd's cloak
Is not yet alive on my flesh.
     Put down those seeds in your hand.

     In your palm is the secret of waking.
     Unclasp your purple-nailed fingers
     And the wood and the sunlight together
     Shall spring, and make good the world.
     The sounds in the air shall find bodies,
     And a feather shall drift from the pine-top
     You shall feel, with your long-buried hand.
     In your palm is the secret of waking,

For the king's grave turns him to light.
A woman shall look through the window

And see me here, huddled and blazing.
My child, mouth open, still sleeping,
Hears the song in the egg of a bird.
The sun shall have told him that song
Of a father returning from darkness,
For the king's grave turns you to light.

All dark is now no more.
In your palm is the secret of waking.
Put down those seeds in your hand;
All Presences change into trees.
A feather shall drift from the pine-top.
The sun shall have told you this song,
For this is the grave of the king;
For the king's grave turns you to light.

I lay at the edge of a well,
And thought how to bury my smile
Under the thorn, where the leaf,
At the sill of oblivion safe,
Put forth its instant green
In a flow from underground.
I sought how the spirit could fall
Down this moss-feathered well:
The motion by which my face
Could descend through structureless grass,
Dreaming of love, and pass
Through solid earth, to rest
On the unseen water's breast,
Timelessly smiling, and free
Of the world, of light, and of me.
I made and imagined that smile
To float there, mile on mile
Of streaming, unknowable wonder,
Overhearing a silence like thunder
Possess every stone of the well
Forever, where my face fell
From the upper, springtime world,
And my odd, living mouth unfurled
An eternal grin, while I
In the bright and stunned grass lay
And turned to air without age.
My first love fingered a page
And sang with Campion.
The heart in my breast turned green;
I entered the words afresh,
At one with her singing flesh.
But all the time I felt
The secret triumph melt
Down through the rooted thorn,
And the smile I filtered through stone
Motionless lie, not murmuring
But listening only, and hearing
My image of joy flow down.

I turned from the girl I had found
In a song once sung by my mother,
And loved my one true brother,
The tall cadaver, who
Either grew or did not grow,
But smiled, with the smile of singing,
Or a smile of incredible longing
To rise through a circle of stone,
Gazing up at a sky, alone
Visible, at the top of a well,
And seeking for years to deliver
His mouth from the endless river
Of my oil-on-the-water smile,
And claim his own grave face
That mine might live in its place.
I lay at the edge of a well;
And then I smiled, and fell.

Except when he enters my son,
The same age as he at his death,
I cannot bring my brother to myself.
I do not have his memory in my life,
Yet he is in my mind and on my hands.
I weave the trivial string upon a light
Dead before I was born.

Mark how the brother must live,
Who comes through the words of my mother.
I have been told he lay
In his death-bed singing with fever,
Performing with string on his fingers
Incredible feats of construction
There before he was born.

His Jacob's Coffin now
Floats deeply between my fingers.
The strings with my thin bones shake.
My eyes go from me, and down
Through my bound, spread hands
To the dead, from the kin of the dead,
Dead before I was born.

The gaze of genius comes back.
The rose-window of Chartres is in it,
And Diogenes' lines upon sand,
And the sun through the Brooklyn Bridge,
And, caught in a web, the regard
Of a skeletal, blood-sharing child
Dead before I was born.

I believe in my father and mother
Finding no hope in these lines.
Out of grief, I was myself
Conceived, and brought to life
To replace the incredible child
Who built on this string in a fever
Dead before I was born.

A man, I make the same forms
For my son, that my brother made,
Who learnt them going to Heaven:
The coffin of light, the bridge,
The cup and saucer of pure air,
Cradle of Cat, the Foot of a Crow
Dead before I was born.

I raise up the bridge and the tower.
I burn the knit coffin in sunlight
For the child who has woven this city:
Who loved, doing this, to die:
Who thought like a spider, and sang,
And completed the maze of my fingers,
Dead before I was born.

Just after the sun
Has closed, I swing the fresh paint of the door
And have opened the new, green dark.
From my house and my silent folk
I step, and lay me in ritual down.

One night each April
I unroll the musty sleeping-bag
And beat from it a cloud of sleeping moths.
I leave the house, which leaves
Its window-light on the ground

In gold frames picturing grass,
And lie in the unconsecrated grove
Of small, suburban pines,
And never move, as the ground not ever shall move,
Remembering, remembering to feel

The still earth turn my house around the sun
Where all is dark, unhoped-for, and undone.
I cannot sleep until the lights are out,
And the lights of the house of grass, also,
Snap off, from underground.

Beneath the gods and animals of Heaven,
Mismade inspiringly, like them,
I fall to a colored sleep
Enveloping the house, or coming out
Of the dark side of the sun,

And begin to believe a dream
I never once have had,
Of being part of the acclaimed rebirth
Of the ruined, calm world, in spring,
When the drowned god and the dreamed-of sun

Unite, to bring the red, the blue,
The common yellow flower out of earth
Of the tended and untended garden: when the chosen man,
Hacked apart in the growing cold
Of the year, by the whole of mindless nature is assembled

From the trembling, untroubled river.
I believe I become that man, become
As bloodless as a god, within the water,
Who yet returns to walk a woman's rooms
Where flowers on the mantel-piece are those

Bought by his death. A warm wind springs
From the curtains. Blue china and milk on the table
Are mild, convincing, and strange.
At that time it is light,
And, as my eyelid lifts

An instant before the other, the last star is withdrawn
Alive, from its fiery fable.
I would not think to move,
Nor cry, "I live," just yet,
Nor shake the twinkling horsehair of my head,

Nor rise, nor shine, nor live
With any but the slant, green, mummied light
And wintry, bell-swung undergloom of waters
Wherethrough my severed head has prophesied
For the silent daffodil and righteous

Leaf, and now has told the truth.
This is the time foresaid, when I must enter
The waking house, and return to a human love
Cherished on faith through winter:
That time when I in the night

Of water lay, with sparkling animals of light
And distance made, with gods
Which move through Heaven only as the spheres
Are moved: by music, music.
Mother, son, and wife

Who live with me: I am in death
And waking. Give me the looks that recall me.
None knows why you have waited
In the cold, thin house for winter
To turn the inmost sunlight green

And blue and red with life,
But it must be so, since you have set
These flowers upon the table, and milk for him
Who, recurring in this body, bears you home
Magnificent pardon, and dread, impending crime.

THE ENCLOSURE

Down the track of a Philippine Island
We rode to the aircraft in trucks,
Going past an enclosure of women,
Those nurses from sick-tents,
With a fume of sand-dust at our backs.
We leapt to the tail-gate,
And drew back, then,
From the guards of the trembling compound,

Where the nailed wire sang like a jew's-harp,
And the women like prisoners paced.
In the dog-panting night-fighter climbing,
Held up between the engines like a child,
I rested my head on my hands;
The drained mask fell from my face.
I thought I could see
Through the dark and the heart-pulsing wire,

Their dungarees float to the floor,
And their light-worthy hair shake down
In curls and remarkable shapes
That the heads of men cannot grow,
And women stand deep in a ring
Of light, and whisper in panic unto us
To deliver them out
Of the circle of impotence, formed

As moonlight spins round a propeller,
Delicate, eternal, though roaring.
A man was suspended above them,
Outcrying the engines with lust.
He was carried away without damage,
And the women, inviolate, woke
In a cloud of gauze,
Overhearing the engines' matched thunder.

Then, the voice of the man, inmixed,
Seemed to them reassuring, unheard-of,

Passing out softly into the hush
Of nipa-leaves, reeds and the sea,
And the long wind up from the beaches,
All making the nets to be trembling
Purely around them,
And fading the desperate sound

To the whine of mosquitoes, turned back
By the powdery cloth that they slept in,
Not touching it, sleeping or waking,
With a thing, not even their hair.
The man sat away in the moonlight,
In a braced, iron, kingly chair,
As the engines labored
And carried him off like a child

To the west, and the thunderstruck mainland.
It may have been the notion of a circle
Of light, or the sigh of the never-thumbed wire,
Or a cry with the shape of propellers,
Or the untouched and breath-trembling nets,
That led me later, at peace,
To shuck off my clothes
In a sickness of moonlight and patience,

With a tongue that cried low, like a jew's-harp,
And a white gaze shimmered upon me
Like an earthless moon, as from women
Sleeping kept from themselves, and beyond me,
To sweat as I did, to the north:
To pray to a skylight of paper, and fall⁻
On the enemy's women
With intact and incredible love.

THE JEWEL

Forgetting I am alive, the tent comes over me
Like grass, and dangling its light on a thread,
Turning the coffee-urn green
Where the boys upon camp-stools are sitting,
   Alone, in late night.

I see my coffee curving in a cup,
A blind, steeled, brimming smile
I hold up alive in my hand.
I smile back a smile I was issued,
   Alone, in late night.

A man doubled strangely in time,
I am waiting to walk with a flashlight
Beam, as a third, weak, drifting leg
To the aircraft standing in darkness,
   Alone, in late night.

Who packs himself into a cockpit
Suspended on clod-hopping wheels,
With the moon held still in the tail-booms,
Has taken his own vow of silence,
   Alone, in late night.

Across from him, someone snaps on
The faceted lights of a cabin.
There, like the meaning of war, he sees
A strong, poor diamond of light,
   Alone, in late night,

And inside it, a man leaning forward
In a helmet, a mask of rubber,
In the balance of a great, stressed jewel
Going through his amazing procedure,
   Alone, in late night.

Truly, do I live? Or shall I die, at last,
Of waiting? Why should the fear grow loud
With the years, of being the first to give in
To the matched, priceless glow of the engines,
    Alone, in late night?

THE PERFORMANCE

The last time I saw Donald Armstrong
He was staggering oddly off into the sun,
Going down, of the Philippine Islands.
I let my shovel fall, and put that hand
Above my eyes, and moved some way to one side
That his body might pass through the sun,

And I saw how well he was not
Standing there on his hands,
On his spindle-shanked forearms balanced,
Unbalanced, with his big feet looming and waving
In the great, untrustworthy air
He flew in each night, when it darkened.

Dust fanned in scraped puffs from the earth
Between his arms, and blood turned his face inside out,
To demonstrate its suppleness
Of veins, as he perfected his role.
Next day, he toppled his head off
On an island beach to the south,

And the enemy's two-handed sword
Did not fall from anyone's hands
At that miraculous sight,
As the head rolled over upon
Its wide-eyed face, and fell
Into the inadequate grave

He had dug for himself, under pressure.
Yet I put my flat hand to my eyebrows
Months later, to see him again
In the sun, when I learned how he died,
And imagined him, there,
Come, judged, before his small captors,

Doing all his lean tricks to amaze them—
The back somersault, the kip-up—
And at last, the stand on his hands,

Perfect, with his feet together,
His head down, evenly breathing,
As the sun poured up from the sea

And the headsman broke down
In a blaze of tears, in that light
Of the thin, long human frame
Upside down in its own strange joy,
And, if some other one had not told him,
Would have cut off the feet

Instead of the head,
And if Armstrong had not presently risen
In kingly, round-shouldered attendance,
And then knelt down in himself
Beside his hacked, glittering grave, having done
All things in this life that he could.

THE WEDDING

During that long time, in those places,
Courage did no hard thing
That could not be easily lived-with.
There, as I watched them have it,
One of them leaned
Low in the bell-tent,
Sewing a tiger's gold head

To the scarred leather breast of his jacket.
Another pounded softly, with a hammer,
A Dutch coin, making a ring for his wife.
In the late afternoon, they placed
The mallet by the pole
Of the slack tent,
And put on the tiger's head, blazing

Over the heart. Among them I moved,
Doing the same, feeling the heavenly beast,
Without a body, attempt in pure terror to move
His legs, as if to spring from us,
His lips, as if
To speak for us,
As we rode to the black-painted aircraft,

And climbed inside and took off.
Many are dead, who fell battling
The gold, helpless beast that lay
Bodiless, on their breaths
Like an angel
In the air,
Who wore their silver rings upon

Their gloved, sprung little fingers,
So precious had they become,
So full of the thought of their wives

That the scratched, tired, beaten-out shining
Was more
Humanly constant
Than they. Years later, I go feeling

All of them turn into heroes,
As in the closed palm of my hand,
And am strangely delighted to find
That they are, to history also,
Heroes as well,
Though nameless,
As the tiger dies, folded over itself in the attic,

As the moon-glowing, center-bored rings
We made good before the dark missions,
Softly pounding our handful of money,
Have been given safely to children,
Or nothing,
Or to the sea,
The human silver, essential to hope in the islands,

Now never worn by woman in its life.

THE OTHER

Holding onto myself by the hand,
I change places into the spirit
I had as a rack-ribbed child,
And walk slowly out through my mind
To the wood, as into a falling fire
Where I turned from that strength-haunted body
Half-way to bronze, as I wished to:

Where I slung up the too-heavy ax-head
And prayed to my thunderous ear-drums
That the deep sweat fall with the leaves
And raise up a man's shape upon me,
Come forth from the work of my arms
And the great, dead tree I hit down on:
That the chicken-chested form I belabored

Might swell with the breast of a statue
From out of the worm-shattered bole,
While I talked all the time through my teeth
To another, unlike me, beside me:
To a brother or king-sized shadow
Who looked at me, burned, and believed me:
Who believed I would rise like Apollo

With armor-cast shoulders upon me:
Whose voice, whistling back through my teeth,
Counted strokes with the hiss of a serpent.
Where the sun through the bright wood drove
Him, mute, and floating strangely, to the ground,
He led me into his house, and sat
Upright, with a face I could never imagine,

With a great harp leant on his shoulder,
And began in deep handfuls to play it:
A sail strung up on its spirit
Gathered up in a ruin in his arms,

That the dog-tired soul might sing
Of the hero, withheld by its body,
Upsprung like a magical man

To a dying, autumnal sound.
As I stood in the shadow-ruled clearing,
Wind died, all over a thicket.
Leaves stood everywhere within falling,
And I thought of our taking the harp
To the tree I had battered to pieces
Many times, many days, in a fever,

With my slow-motion, moon-sided ax.
Reason fell from my mind at a touch
Of the cords, and the dead tree leapt
From the ground, and together, and alive.
I thought of my body to come;
My mind burst into that green.
My brother rose beside me from the earth,

With the wing-bone of music on his back
Trembling strongly with heartfelt gold,
And ascended like a bird into the tree,
And music fell in a comb, as I stood
In a bull's heavy, bronze-bodied shape
As it mixed with a god's, on the ground,
And leaned on the helve of the ax.

Now, owing my arms to the dead
Tree, and the leaf-loosing, mortal wood,
Still hearing that music amaze me,
I walk through the time-stricken forest,
And wish another body for my life,
Knowing that none is given
By the giant, unusable tree

And the leaf-shaped lightning of sun,
And rail at my lust of self
With an effort like chopping through root-stocks:

Yet the light, looming brother but more
Brightly above me is blazing,
In that music come down from the branches
In utter, unseasonable glory,

Telling nothing but how I made
By hand, a creature to keep me dying
Years longer, and coming to sing in the wood
Of what love still might give,
Could I turn wholly mortal in my mind,
My body-building angel give me rest,
This tree cast down its foliage with the years.

Many trees can stand unshaded
In this place where the sun is alone,
But some may break out.
They may be taken to Heaven,
So gold is my only sight.

Through me, two red cows walk;
From a crowning glory
Of slowness they are not taken.
Let one hoof knock on a stone,
And off it a spark jump quickly,

And fire may sweep these fields,
And all outburn the blind sun.
Like a new light I enter my life,
And hover, not yet consumed,
With the trees in holy alliance,

About to be offered up,
About to get wings where we stand.
The whole field stammers with gold;
No leaf but is actively still;
There is no quiet or noise;

Continually out of a fire
A bull walks forth,
And makes of my mind a red beast
At each step feeling how
The sun more deeply is burning

Because trees and cattle exist.
I go away, in the end.
In the shade, my bull's horns die
From my head; in some earthly way
I have been given my heart:

Behind my back, a tree leaps up
On wings that could save me from death.
Its branches dance over my head.
Its flight strikes a root in me.
A cow beneath it lies down.

Feeling it with me
On it, barely float, the narrow plank on the water,
I stepped from the clam-shell beach,
Breaking in nearly down through the sun
Where it lay on the sea,
And poled off, gliding upright
Onto the shining topsoil of the bay.

Later, it came to be said
That I was seen walking on water,
Not moving my legs
Except for the wrong step of sliding:
A child who leaned on a staff,
A curious pilgrim hiking
Between two open blue worlds,

My motion a miracle,
Leaving behind me no footprint,
But only the shimmering place
Of an infinite step upon water
In which sat still and were shining
Many marsh-birds and pelicans.
Alongside my feet, the shark

Lay buried and followed,
His eyes on my childish heels.
Thus, taking all morning to stalk
From one littered beach to another,
I came out on land, and dismounted,
Making marks in the sand with my toes
Which truly had walked there, on water,

With the pelicans beating their shadows
Through the mirror carpet
Down, and the shark pursuing
The boy on the burning deck

Of a bare single ship-wrecked board.
Shoving the plank out to sea, I walked
Inland, on numb sparkling feet,

With the sun on the sea unbroken,
Nor the long quiet step of the miracle
Doing anything behind me but blazing,
With the birds in it nodding their heads,
That must ponder that footstep forever,
Rocking, or until I return
In my ghost, which shall have become, then,

A boy with a staff,
To loose them, beak and feather, from the spell
Laid down by a balancing child,
Unstable, tight-lipped, and amazed,
And, under their place of enthrallment,
A huge, hammer-headed spirit
Shall pass, as if led by the nose into Heaven.

AWAITING THE SWIMMER

Light fails, in crossing a river.
The current shines deeply without it.
I hold a white cloth in my hands.
The air turns over one leaf.
One force is left in my arms
To handle the cloth, spread it gently,
And show where I stand above water.

I see her loosed hair straining.
She is trying to come to me, here.
I cannot swim, and she knows it.
Her gaze makes the cloth burn my hands.
I can stand only where I am standing.
Shall she fail, and go down to the sea?
Shall she call, as she changes to water?

She swims to overcome fear.
One force is left in her arms.
How can she come, but in glory?
The current burns; I love
That moving-to-me love, now passing
The midst of the road where she's buried.
Her best motions come from the river;

Her fear flows away to the sea.
The way to move upon water
Is to work lying down, as in love.
The way to wait in a field
Is to hold a white cloth in your hands
And sing with the sound of the river.
Called here by the luminous towel,

My rib-humming breath, and my love,
She steps from the twilit water.
At the level of my throat, she closes
Her eyes, and ends my singing.

I wrap her thin form in the towel,
And we walk through the motionless grasses
To the house, where the chairs we sit in

Have only one force in their arms.
The bed like the river is shining.
Yet what shall I do, when I reach her
Through the moon opened wide on the floor-boards?
What can I perform, to come near her?
How hope to bear up, when she gives me
The fear-killing moves of her body?

ON THE HILL BELOW THE LIGHTHOUSE

Now I can be sure of my sleep;
I have lost the blue sea in my eyelids.
From a place in the mind too deep
For thought, a light like a wind is beginning.
        Now I can be sure of my sleep.

When the moon is held strongly within it,
The eye of the mind opens gladly.
Day changes to dark, and is bright,
And miracles trust to the body,
        When the moon is held strongly within it.

A woman comes true when I think her.
Her eyes on the window are closing.
She has dressed the stark wood of a chair.
Her form and my body are facing.
        A woman comes true when I think her.

Shade swings, and she lies against me.
The lighthouse has opened its brain.
A browed light travels the sea.
Her clothes on the chair spread their wings.
        Shade swings, and she lies against me.

Let us lie in returning light,
As a bright arm sweeps through the moon.
The sun is dead, thinking of night
Swung round like a thing on a chain.
        Let us lie in returning light.

Let us lie where your angel is walking
In shadow, from wall onto wall,
Cast forth from your off-cast clothing
To pace the dim room where we fell.
        Let us lie where your angel is walking,

Coming back, coming back, going over.
An arm turns the light world around

The dark. Again we are waiting to hover
In a blaze in the mind like a wind
    Coming back, coming back, going over.

    Now I can be sure of my sleep;
    The moon is held strongly within it.
    A woman comes true when I think her.
    Shade swings, and she lies against me.
    Let us lie in returning light;
    Let us lie where your angel is walking,
    Coming back, coming back, going over.

It may be the sea-moving moon
Is swayed upon the waves by what I do.
I make on the night no shade,
But a small-stepping sound upon water.
I have rowed toward the moon for miles,
Till the lights upon shore have been blown

Slowly out by my infinite breath,
By distance come slowly as age,
And at last, on the heart-shaken boards
Of the boat, I lie down,
Beginning to sleep, sustained
By a huge, ruined stone in the sky

As it draws the lost tide-water flat,
And the wind springs into the sea,
And for miles on the calming surface
The moon creeps into its image.
Inside the one flame of that stone
My breath sheds the light of the sun,

All water shines down out of Heaven,
And the things upon shore that I love
Are immortal, inescapable, there.
I know one human love,
And soon it must find me out.
I shall float in the mind of a woman

Till the sun takes its breath from my mouth,
And whispers to my wife upon the land,
Who, like this unbalancing light,
When the half-eaten stone in the sky
Pulls evenly, and the wind leaps out of its life,
Assembles upon this place,

And finds me exultantly sleeping,
My ear going down to the floor
Of the sea, overhearing, not fish,

Their gills like a bracken all swaying,
But man and wife breathing together.
I shall row from the sun to the beach,

Where she shall have risen from darkness,
From her vast, shining place in the moonlight,
Where a man slaved for hours to reach her
And lie in the quick of her image.
She shall stand to her knees in her shadow,
Gazing outward, her eyes unshaded,

As I ride blindly home from the sun,
Not wishing to know how she came there,
Commanded by glorious powers:
At night by the night's one stone
Laid openly on the lost waves,
By her eyes catching fire in the morning.

On the way to a woman, I give
My heart all the way into moonlight.
Now down from all sides it is beating.
The moon turns around in the fix
If its light; its other side totally shines.
Like the dead, I have newly arisen,
Amazed by the light I can throw.
Stand waiting, my love, where you are,

For slowly amazed I come forward
From my bed through the land between,
Through the stone held in air by my heartbeat.
My thin flesh is shed by my shadow;
My hair has turned white with a thought.
No thing that shall die as I step
May fall, or not sing of rebirth.
Very far from myself I come toward you

In the fire of the sun, dead-locked
With the moon's new face in its glory.
I see by the dark side of light.
I am he who I should have become.
A bird that has died overhead
Sings a song to sustain him forever.
Elsewhere I have dreamed of my birth,
And come from my death as I dreamed;

Each time, the moon has burned backward.
Each time, my heart has gone from me
And shaken the sun from the moonlight.
Each time, a woman has called,
And my breath come to life in her singing.
Once more I come home from my ghost.
I give up my father and mother;
My own love has raised up my limbs:

I take my deep heart from the air.
The road like a woman is singing.
It sings with what makes my heart beat
In the air, and the moon turn around.
The dead have their chance in my body.
The stars are drawn into their myths.
I bear nothing but moonlight upon me.
I am known; I know my love.

Drowning With Others

To Maxine, Christopher, and Kevin

I

In a stable of boats I lie still,
From all sleeping children hidden.
The leap of a fish from its shadow
Makes the whole lake instantly tremble.
With my foot on the water, I feel
The moon outside

Take on the utmost of its power.
I rise and go out through the boats.
I set my broad sole upon silver,
On the skin of the sky, on the moonlight,
Stepping outward from earth onto water
In quest of the miracle

This village of children believed
That I could perform as I dived
For one who had sunk from my sight.
I saw his cropped haircut go under.
I leapt, and my steep body flashed
Once, in the sun.

Dark drew all the light from my eyes.
Like a man who explores his death
By the pull of his slow-moving shoulders,
I hung head down in the cold,
Wide-eyed, contained, and alone
Among the weeds,

And my fingertips turned into stone
From clutching immovable blackness.
Time after time I leapt upward
Exploding in breath, and fell back
From the change in the children's faces
At my defeat.

Drowning With Others 51

Beneath them I swam to the boathouse
With only my life in my arms
To wait for the lake to shine back
At the risen moon with such power
That my steps on the light of the ripples
Might be sustained.

Beneath me is nothing but brightness
Like the ghost of a snowfield in summer.
As I move toward the center of the lake,
Which is also the center of the moon,
I am thinking of how I may be
The savior of one

Who has already died in my care.
The dark trees fade from around me.
The moon's dust hovers together.
I call softly out, and the child's
Voice answers through blinding water.
Patiently, slowly,

He rises, dilating to break
The surface of stone with his forehead.
He is one I do not remember
Having ever seen in his life.
The ground I stand on is trembling
Upon his smile.

I wash the black mud from my hands.
On a light given off by the grave
I kneel in the quick of the moon
At the heart of a distant forest
And hold in my arms a child
Of water, water, water.

When in that gold
Of fires, quietly sitting
With the men whose brothers are hounds,

You hear the first tone
Of a dog on scent, you look from face
To face, to see whose will light up.

When that light comes
Inside the dark light of the fire,
You know which chosen man has heard

A thing like his own dead
Speak out in a marvelous, helpless voice
That he has been straining to hear.

Miles away in the dark,
His enchanted dog can sense
How his features glow like a savior's,

And begins to hunt
In a frenzy of desperate pride.
Among us, no one's eyes give off a light

For the red fox
Playing in and out of his scent,
Leaping stones, doubling back over water.

Who runs with the fox
Must sit here like his own image,
Giving nothing of himself

To the sensitive flames,
With no human joy rising up,
Coming out of his face to be seen.

And it is hard,

When the fox leaps into his burrow,
To keep that singing down,

To sit with the fire
Drawn into one's secret features,
And all eyes turning around

From the dark wood
Until they come, amazed, upon
A face that does not shine

Back from itself,
That holds its own light and takes more,
Like the face of the dead, sitting still,

Giving no sign,
Making no outcry, no matter
Who may be straining to hear.

Being his resting place,
I do not even tense
The muscles of a leg
Or I would seem to be changing.
Instead, I turn the page
Of the notebook, carefully not

Remembering what I have written,
For now, with my feet beneath him
Dying like embers,
The poem is beginning to move
Up through my pine-prickling legs
Out of the night wood,

Taking hold of the pen by my fingers.
Before me the fox floats lightly,
On fire with his holy scent.
All, all are running.
Marvelous is the pursuit,
Like a dazzle of nails through the ankles,

Like a twisting shout through the trees
Sent after the flying fox
Through the holes of logs, over streams
Stock-still with the pressure of moonlight.
My killed legs,
My legs of a dead thing, follow,

Quick as pins, through the forest,
And all rushes on into dark
And ends on the brightness of paper.
When my hand, which speaks in a daze
The hypnotized language of beasts,
Shall falter, and fail

Back into the human tongue,
And the dog gets up and goes out
To wander the dawning yard,

I shall crawl to my human bed
And lie there smiling at sunrise,
With the scent of the fox

Burning my brain like an incense,
Floating out of the night wood,
Coming home to my wife and my sons
From the dream of an animal,
Assembling the self I must wake to,
Sleeping to grow back my legs.

No water is still, on top.
Without wind, even, it is full
Of a chill, superficial agitation.
It is easy to forget,
Or not to know at all

That fish do not move
By means of this rippling
Along the outside of water, or
By anything touching on air.
Where they are, it is still,

Under a wooden bridge,
Under the poised oar
Of a boat, while the rower leans
And blows his mistaken breath
To make the surface shake,

Or yells at it, or sings,
Half believing the brilliant scan
Of ripples will carry the fish away
On his voice like a buried wind.
Or it may be that a fish

Is simply lying under
The ocean-broad sun
Which comes down onto him
Like a tremendous, suffusing
Open shadow

Of gold, where nothing is,
Sinking into the water,
Becoming dark around
His body. Where he is now
Could be gold mixed

With absolute blackness.
The surface at mid-sea shivers,

But he does not feel it
Like a breath, or like anything.
Yet suddenly his frame shakes,

Convulses the whole ocean
Under the trivial, quivering
Surface, and he is
Hundreds of feet away,
Still picking up speed, still shooting

Through half-gold,
Going nowhere. Nothing sees him.
One must think of this to understand
The instinct of fear and trembling,
And, of its one movement, the depth.

Here they are. The soft eyes open.
If they have lived in a wood
It is a wood.
If they have lived on plains
It is grass rolling
Under their feet forever.

Having no souls, they have come,
Anyway, beyond their knowing.
Their instincts wholly bloom
And they rise.
The soft eyes open.

To match them, the landscape flowers,
Outdoing, desperately
Outdoing what is required:
The richest wood,
The deepest field.

For some of these,
It could not be the place
It is, without blood.
These hunt, as they have done,
But with claws and teeth grown perfect,

More deadly than they can believe.
They stalk more silently,
And crouch on the limbs of trees,
And their descent
Upon the bright backs of their prey

May take years
In a sovereign floating of joy.
And those that are hunted
Know this as their life,
Their reward: to walk

Under such trees in full knowledge
Of what is in glory above them,
And to feel no fear,
But acceptance, compliance.
Fulfilling themselves without pain

At the cycle's center,
They tremble, they walk
Under the tree,
They fall, they are torn,
They rise, they walk again.

Inventing a story with grass,
I find a young horse deep inside it.
I cannot nail wires around him;
My fence posts fail to be solid,

And he is free, strangely, without me.
With his head still browsing the greenness,
He walks slowly out of the pasture
To enter the sun of his story.

My mind freed of its own creature,
I find myself deep in my life
In a room with my child and my mother,
When I feel the sun climbing my shoulder

Change, to include a new horse.

FOG ENVELOPS THE ANIMALS

Fog envelops the animals.
Not one can be seen, and they live.
At my knees, a cloud wears slowly
Up out of the buried earth.
In a white suit I stand waiting.

Soundlessly whiteness is eating
My visible self alive.
I shall enter this world like the dead,
Floating through tree trunks on currents
And streams of untouchable pureness

That shine without thinking of light.
My hands burn away at my sides
In the pale, risen ghosts of deep rivers.
In my hood peaked like a flame,
I feel my own long-hidden,

Long-sought invisibility
Come forth from my solid body.
I stand with all beasts in a cloud.
Of them I am deadly aware,
And they not of me, in this life.

Only my front teeth are showing
As the dry fog mounts to my lips
In a motion long buried in water,
And now, one by one, my teeth
Like rows of candles go out.

In the spirit of flame, my hood
Holds the face of my soul without burning,
And I drift forward
Through the hearts of the curdling oak trees,
Borne by the river of Heaven.

My arrows, keener than snowflakes,
Are with me whenever I touch them.
Above my head, the trees exchange their arms
In the purest fear upon earth.
Silence. Whiteness. Hunting.

THE SUMMONS

For something out of sight,
I cup a grass-blade in my hands,
Tasting the root, and blow.
I speak to the wind, and it lives.
No hunter has taught me this call;
It comes out of childhood and playgrounds.
I hang my longbow on a branch.
The wind at my feet extends

Quickly out, across the lake,
Containing the sound I have made.
The water below me becomes
Bright ploughland in its body.
I breathe on my thumbs, and am blowing
A horn that encircles the forest.
Across the lake, a tree
Now thrums in tremendous cadence.

Beneath it, some being stumbles,
And answers me slowly and greatly
With a tongue as rasping as sawgrass.
I lower my hands, and I listen
To the beast that shall die of its love.
I sound my green trumpet again,
And the whole wood sings in my palms.
The vast trees are tuned to my bowstring

And the deep-rooted voice I have summoned.
I have carried it here from a playground
Where I rolled in the grass with my brothers.
Nothing moves, but something intends to.
The water that puffed like a wing
Is one flattened blaze through the branches.
Something falls from the bank, and is swimming.
My voice turns around me like foliage,

And I pluck my longbow off the limb
Where it shines with a musical light,
And crouch within death, awaiting
The beast in the water, in love
With the palest and gentlest of children,
Whom the years have turned deadly with knowledge:
Who summons him forth, and now
Pulls wide the great, thoughtful arrow.

IN THE TREE HOUSE AT NIGHT

And now the green household is dark.
The half-moon completely is shining
On the earth-lighted tops of the trees.
To be dead, a house must be still.
The floor and the walls wave me slowly;
I am deep in them over my head.
The needles and pine cones about me

Are full of small birds at their roundest,
Their fists without mercy gripping
Hard down through the tree to the roots
To sing back at light when they feel it.
We lie here like angels in bodies,
My brothers and I, one dead,
The other asleep from much living,

In mid-air huddled beside me.
Dark climbed to us here as we climbed
Up the nails I have hammered all day
Through the sprained, comic rungs of the ladder
Of broom handles, crate slats, and laths
Foot by foot up the trunk to the branches
Where we came out at last over lakes

Of leaves, of fields disencumbered of earth
That move with the moves of the spirit.
Each nail that sustains us I set here;
Each nail in the house is now steadied
By my dead brother's huge, freckled hand.
Through the years, he has pointed his hammer
Up into these limbs, and told us

That we must ascend, and all lie here.
Step after step he has brought me,
Embracing the trunk as his body,
Shaking its limbs with my heartbeat,
Till the pine cones danced without wind

And fell from the branches like apples.
In the arm-slender forks of our dwelling

I breathe my live brother's light hair.
The blanket around us becomes
As solid as stone, and it sways.
With all my heart, I close
The blue, timeless eye of my mind.
Wind springs, as my dead brother smiles
And touches the tree at the root;

A shudder of joy runs up
The trunk; the needles tingle;
One bird uncontrollably cries.
The wind changes round, and I stir
Within another's life. Whose life?
Who is dead? Whose presence is living?
When may I fall strangely to earth,

Who am nailed to this branch by a spirit?
Can two bodies make up a third?
To sing, must I feel the world's light?
My green, graceful bones fill the air
With sleeping birds. Alone, alone
And with them I move gently.
I move at the heart of the world.

FOR THE NIGHTLY ASCENT OF THE HUNTER ORION
OVER A FOREST CLEARING

Now secretness dies of the open.
Yet all around, all over, night
Things are waking fast,
Waking with all their power.
Who can arise

From his dilating shadow
When one foot is longing to tiptoe
And the other to take the live
Stand of a tree that belongs here?
As the owl's gaze

Most slowly begins to create
Its sight from the death of the sun,
As the mouse feels the whole wood turn
The gold of the owl's new eyes,
And the fox moves

Out of the ground where he sleeps,
No man can stand upright
And drag his body forth
Through an open space in the foliage
Unless he rises

As does the hunter Orion,
Thinking to cross a blue hollow
Through the dangers of twilight,
Feeling that he must run
And that he will

Take root forever and stand,
Does both at once, and neither,
Grows blind, and then sees everything,
Steps and becomes a man
Of stars instead,

Who from invisibility
Has come, arranged in the light
Of himself, revealed tremendously
In his fabulous, rigid, eternal
Unlooked-for role.

THE OWL KING

I

THE CALL

Through the trees, with the moon underfoot,
More soft than I can, I call.
I hear the king of the owls sing
Where he moves with my son in the gloom.
My tongue floats off in the darkness.
I feel the deep dead turn
My blind child round toward my calling,
Through the trees, with the moon underfoot,

In a sound I cannot remember.
It whispers like straw in my ear,
And shakes like a stone under water.
My bones stand on tiptoe inside it.
Which part of the sound did I utter?
Is it song, or is half of it whistling?
What spirit has swallowed my tongue?
Or is it a sound I remember?

And yet it is coming back,
Having gone, adrift on its spirit,
Down, over and under the river,
And stood in a ring in a meadow
Round a child with a bird gravely dancing.
I hear the king of the owls sing.
I did not awaken that sound,
And yet it is coming back,

In touching every tree upon the hill.
The breath falls out of my voice,
And yet the singing keeps on.
The owls are dancing, fastened by their toes
Upon the pines. Come, son, and find me here,
In love with the sound of my voice.
Come calling the same soft song,
And touching every tree upon the hill.

II

THE OWL KING

I swore to myself I would see
When all but my seeing had failed.
Every light was too feeble to show
My world as I knew it must be.
At the top of the staring night
I sat on the oak in my shape
With my claws growing deep into wood
And my sight going slowly out
Inch by inch, as into a stone,
Disclosing the rabbits running
Beneath my bent, growing throne,
And the foxes lighting their hair,
And the serpent taking the shape
Of the stream of life as it slept.
When I thought of the floating sound
In which my wings would outspread,
I felt the hooked tufts on my head
Enlarge, and dream like a crown,
And my voice unplaceable grow
Like a feathery sigh;
I could not place it myself.
For years I humped on the tree
Whose leaves held the sun and the moon.
At last I opened my eyes
In the sun, and saw nothing there.
That night I parted my lids
Once more, and saw dark burn
Greater than sunlight or moonlight,
For it burned from deep within me.
The still wood glowed like a brain.
I prised up my claws, and spread
My huge, ashen wings from my body,
For I heard what I listened to hear.
Someone spoke to me out of the distance
In a voice like my own, but softer.
I rose like the moon from the branch.

Through trees at his light touch trembling
The blind child drifted to meet me,
His blue eyes shining like mine.
In a ragged clearing he stopped,
And I circled, beating above him,
Then fell to the ground and hopped
Forward, taking his hand in my claw.
Every tree's life lived in his fingers.
Gravely we trod with each other
As beasts at their own wedding, dance.
Through the forest, the questioning voice
Of his father came to us there,
As though the one voice of us both,
Its high, frightened sound becoming
A perfect, irrelevant music
In which we profoundly moved,
I in the innermost shining
Of my blazing, invented eyes,
And he in the total of dark.
Each night, now, high on the oak,
With his father calling like music,
He sits with me here on the bough,
His eyes inch by inch going forward
Through stone dark, burning and picking
The creatures out one by one,
Each waiting alive in its own
Peculiar light to be found:
The mouse in its bundle of terror,
The fox in the flame of its hair,
And the snake in the form of all life.
Each night he returns to his bed,
To the voice of his singing father,
To dream of the owl king sitting
Alone in the crown of my will.
In my ruling passion, he rests.
All dark shall come to light.

III

THE BLIND CHILD'S STORY

I am playing going down
In my weight lightly,
Down, down the hill.
No one calls me
Out of the air.
The heat is falling
On the backs of my hands
And holding coldness.
They say it shines two ways.
The darkness is great
And luminous in my eyes.
Down I am quickly going;
A leaf falls on me,
It must be a leaf I hear it
Be thin against me, and now
The ground is level,
It moves it is not ground,
My feet flow cold
And wet, and water rushes
Past as I climb out.
I am there, on the other side.
I own the entire world.

It closes a little; the sky
Must be cold, must be giving off
Creatures that stand here.
I say they shine one way.
Trees they are trees around me,
Leaves branches and bark;
I can touch them all; I move
From one to another—someone said
I seem to be blessing them.
I am blessing them
Slowly, one after another
Deeper into the wood.

The dark is changing,
Its living is packed in closer
Overhead—more trees and leaves—
Tremendous. It touches
Something touches my hand,
Smelling it, a cold nose
Of breath, an ear of silk
Is gone. It is here I begin
To call to something unearthly.
Something is here, something before
Me sitting above me
In the wood in a crown,
Its eyes newborn in its head
From the death of the sun.
I can hear it rising on wings.
I hear that fluttering
Cease, and become
Pure soundless dancing
Like leaves not leaves;
Now down out of air
It lumbers to meet me,
Stepping oddly on earth,
Awkwardly, royally.
My father is calling

Through the touched trees;
All distance is weeping and singing.
In my hand I feel
A talon, a grandfather's claw
Bone cold and straining
To keep from breaking my skin.
I know this step, I know it,
And we are deep inside.
My father's voice is over
And under us, sighing.
Nothing is strange where we are.
The huge bird bows and returns,
For I, too, have done the same

As he leads me, rustling,
A pile of leaves in my hands;
The dry feathers shuffle like cards
On his dusty shoulders,
Not touching a tree,
Not brushing the side of a leaf
Or a point of grass.

We stop and stand like bushes.
But my father's music comes
In, goes on, comes in,
Into the wood,
Into the ceased dance.
And now the hard beak whispers
Softly, and we climb
Some steps of bark
Living and climbing with us
Into the leaves.
I sit among leaves,
And the whole branch hums
With the owl's full, weightless power
As he closes his feet on the wood.
My own feet dangle
And tingle down;
My head is pointing
Deep into moonlight,
Deep into branches and leaves,
Directing my blackness there,
The personal dark of my sight,
And now it is turning a color.
My eyes are blue at last.
Something within the place
I look is piled and coiled.
It lifts its head from itself.
Its form is lit, and gives back
What my eyes are giving it freely.
I learn from the master of sight
What to do when the sun is dead,

How to make the great darkness work
As it wants of itself to work.
I feel the tree where we sit
Grow under me, and live.
I may have been here for years;
In the coil, the heaped-up creature
May have taken that long to lift
His head, to break his tongue
From his thin lips,
But he is there. I shut my eyes
And my eyes are gold,
As gold as an owl's,
As gold as a king's.
I open them. Farther off,
Beyond the swaying serpent,
A creature is burning itself
In a smoke of hair through the bushes.
The fox moves; a small thing
Being caught, cries out,
And I understand
How beings and sounds go together;
I understand
The voice of my singing father.
I shall be king of the wood.

Our double throne shall grow
Forever, until I see
The self of every substance
As it crouches, hidden and free.
The owl's face runs with tears
As I take him in my arms
In the glow of original light
Of Heaven. I go down
In my weight lightly down
The tree, and now
Through the soul of the wood
I walk in consuming glory
Past the snake, the fox, and the mouse:

I see as the owl king sees,
By going in deeper than darkness.
The wood comes back in a light
It did not know it withheld,
And I can tell
By its breathing glow
Each tree on which I laid
My hands when I was blind.

I cross the cold-footed flowing,
The creek, a religious fire
Streaming my ankles away,
And climb through the slanted meadow.
My father cannot remember
That he ever lived in this house.
To himself he bays like a hound,
Entranced by the endless beauty
Of his grief-stricken singing and calling.
He is singing simply to moonlight,
Like a dog howling,
And it is holy song
Out of his mouth.
Father, I am coming,
I am here on my own;
I move as you sing,
As if it were Heaven.
It is Heaven. I am walking
To you and seeing
Where I walk home.
What I have touched, I see
With the dark of my blue eyes.
Far off, the owl king
Sings like my father, growing
In power. Father, I touch
Your face. I have not seen
My own, but it is yours.
I come, I advance,
I believe everything, I am here.

II

BETWEEN TWO PRISONERS

I would not wish to sit
In my shape bound together with wire,
Wedged into a child's sprained desk
In the schoolhouse under the palm tree.
Only those who did could have done it.

One bled from a cut on his temple,
And sat with his tousled head bowed,
His wound for him painfully thinking.
A belief in words grew upon them
That the unbound, who walk, cannot know.

The guard at the window leaned close
In a movement he took from the palm tree,
To hear, in a foreign tongue,
All things which cannot be said.
In the splintering clapboard room

They rested the sides of their faces
On the tops of the desks as they talked.
Because of the presence of children
In the deep signs carved in the desk tops,
Signs on the empty blackboard

Began, like a rain, to appear.
In the luminous chalks of all colors,
Green face, yellow breast, white sails
Whose wing feathers made the wall burn
Like a waterfall seen in a fever,

An angel came boldly to light
From his hands casting green, ragged bolts
Each having the shape of a palm leaf.

Also traced upon darkness in chalk
Was the guard at the rear window leaning

Through the red, vital strokes of his tears.
Behind him, men lying with swords
As with women, heard themselves sing,
And woke, then, terribly knowing
That they were a death squad, singing

In its sleep, in the middle of a war.
A wind sprang out of the tree.
The guard awoke by the window,
And found he had talked to himself
All night, in two voices, of Heaven.

He stood in the sunlit playground
Where the quiet boys knelt together
In their bloodletting trusses of wire,
And saw their mussed, severed heads
Make the ground jump up like a dog.

I watched the small guard be hanged
A year later, to the day,
In a closed horse stall in Manila.
No one knows what language he spoke
As his face changed into all colors,

And gave off his red, promised tears,
Or if he learned blindly to read
A child's deep, hacked hieroglyphics
Which can call up an angel from nothing,
Or what was said for an instant, there,

In the tied, scribbled dark, between him
And a figure drawn hugely in chalk,
Speaking words that can never be spoken
Except in a foreign tongue,
In the end, at the end of a war.

ARMOR

When this is the thing you put on
The world is pieced slowly together
In the power of the crab and the insect.
The make of the eyeball changes
As over your mouth you draw down
A bird's bill made for a man.

As your weight upon earth is redoubled
There is no way of standing alone
More, or no way of being
More with the bound, shining dead.
You have put on what you should wear,
Not into the rattling of battle,

But into a silence where nothing
Threatens but Place itself: the shade
Of the forest, the strange, crowned
Motionless sunlight of Heaven,
With the redbird blinking and shooting
Across the nailed beam of the eyepiece.

In that light, in the wood, in armor,
I look in myself for the being
I was in a life before life
In a glade more silent than breathing,
Where I took off my body of metal
Like a brother whose features I knew

By the feel of their strength on my face
And whose limbs by the shining of mine.
In a vision I fasten him there,
The bright locust shell of my strength
Like a hanged man waiting in Heaven,
And then steal off to my life.

In my home, a night nearer death,
I wake with no shield on my breastbone,
Breathing deep through my sides like an insect,

My closed hand falling and rising
Where it lies like the dead on my heart.
I cannot remember my brother;

Before I was born he went from me
Ablaze with the meaning of typhoid.
In a fever I see him turn slowly
Under the strange, perfect branches
Where somehow I left him to wait
That I might be naked on earth,

His crowned face dazzingly closed,
His curving limbs giving off
Pure energy into the leaves.
When I give up my hold on my breath
I long to dress deeply at last
In the gold of my waiting brother

Who shall wake and shine on my limbs
As I walk, made whole, into Heaven.
I shall not remember his face
Or my dazed, eternal one
Until I have opened my hand
And touched the grave glow of his breast

To stop the gaunt turning of metal:
Until I have let the still sun
Down into the stare of the eyepiece
And raised its bird's beak to confront
What man is within to live with me
When I begin living forever.

IN THE LUPANAR AT POMPEII

There are tracks which belong to wheels
Long since turned to air and time.
Those are the powerful chariots
I follow down cobblestones,
Not being dragged, exactly,
But not of my own will, either,
Going past the flower sellers'
And the cindery produce market
And the rich man's home, and the house
Of the man who kept a dog
Set in mosaic.

As tourist, but mostly as lecher,
I seek out the dwelling of women
Who all expect me, still, because
They expect anybody who comes.
I am ready to pay, and I do,
And then go in among them
Where on the dark walls of their home
They hold their eternal postures,
Doing badly drawn, exacting,
Too-willing, wide-eyed things
With dry-eyed art.

I sit down in one of the rooms
Where it happened again and again.
I could be in prison, or dead,
Cast down for my sins in a cell
Still filled with a terrible motion
Like the heaving and sighing of earth
To be free of the heat it restrains.
I feel in my heart how the heart
Of the mountain broke, and the women
Fled onto the damp of the walls
And shaped their embraces

To include whoever would come here
After the stone-cutting chariots.

I think of the marvel of lust
Which can always, at any moment,
Become more than it believed,
And almost always is less:
I think of its possible passing
Beyond, into tender awareness,
Into helplessness, weeping, and death:
It must be like the first
Soft floating of ash,

When, in the world's frankest hands,
Someone lay with his body shaken
Free of the self: that amazement—
For we who must try to explain
Ourselves in the house of this flesh
Never can tell the quick heat
Of our own from another's breathing,
Nor yet from the floating of feathers
That form in our lungs when the mountain
Settles like odd, warm snow against
Our willing limbs.

We never can really tell
Whether nature condemns us or loves us
As we lie here dying of breath
And the painted, unchanging women,
Believing the desperate dead
Where they stripped to the skin of the soul
And whispered to us, as to
Their panting, observing selves:
"Passion. Before we die
Let us hope for no longer
But truly know it."

There are moments a man turns from us
Whom we have all known until now.
Upgathered, we watch him grow,
Unshipping his shoulder bones

Like human, everyday wings
That he has not ever used,
Releasing his hair from his brain,
A kingfisher's crest, confused

By the God-tilted light of Heaven.
His deep, window-watching smile
Comes closely upon us in waves,
And spreads, and now we are

At last within it, dancing.
Slowly we turn and shine
Upon what is holding us,
As under our feet he soars,

Struck dumb as the angel of Eden,
In wide, eye-opening rings.
Yet the hand on my shoulder fears
To feel my own wingblades spring,

To feel me sink slowly away
In my hair turned loose like a thought
Of a fisherbird dying in flight.
If I opened my arms, I could hear

Every shell in the sea find the word
It has tried to put into my mouth.
Broad flight would become of my dancing,
And I would obsess the whole sea,

But I keep rising and singing
With my last breath. Upon my back,

With his hand on my unborn wing,
A man rests easy as sunlight

Who has kept himself free of the forms
Of the deaf, down-soaring dead,
And me laid out and alive
For nothing at all, in his arms.

III

DOVER: BELIEVING IN KINGS

As we drove down the ramp from the boat
The sun flashed once
Or through hand-shieldedly twice;
In a silence out of a sound
We watched for channel swimmers dim with grease,
Come, here, to the ale of the shallows.
Within a wind, a wind sprang slowly up.
Birds hovered where they were.
As they were there, the airstream of the cliffs
Overcame, came over them
In the sackcloth and breast-beating gray
The king wears newly, at evening.
In a movement you cannot imagine
Of air, the gulls fall, shaken.

No stronger than the teeth in my head
Or a word laid bare
On chilling glass, the breathed stone over us rode.
From its top, the eye may sail,
Outgrowing the graven nerves
Of the brow's long-thought-out lines,
To France, on its own color.
From a child's tall book, I knew this place
The child must believe, with the king:
Where, doubtless, now, lay lovers
Restrained by a cloud, and the moon
Into force coming justly, above.
In a movement you cannot imagine
Of love, the gulls fall, mating.

We stopped; the birds hung up their arms
Inside the wind
So that they heeled; above, around us,
Their harp-strung feathers made

The sound, quickly mortal, of sighing.
We watched them in pure obsession.
Where they did move, we moved
Along the cliffs, the promenade,
The walls, the pebble beach,
And felt the inmost island turn,
In their cross-cut, wing-walking cries,
To a thing, as weeping, felt,
And haunted by the balancement of light
The king wears newly, in singing.

We wandered off from the car
In the light, half-sun,
Half-moon, in a worn-down shine out of stone,
And the taste of an iron ladle on the wind.
In the moon's grimed, thumbprint silver
The anchor spoke through the bell,
Far out, the hour that hung in the sea.
I threw a slow-flying stone; it dropped
Inside the brilliant echo of a light.
In a great, clustered, overdrawn sigh
The gulls went up, on a raiment of wings
The king wears newly, in panic.
In a movement you cannot imagine
Of error, the gulls rise, wholly.

We climbed a wall they had flown.
Each light below
On water, shook like a thing in a lathe.
In the heron crest of a lamp,
Among lights, in their treading motion,
The head of my reflection seemed to sing
A dark, quickened side of the truth.
I touched my wife. I saw my son, unborn,
Left living after me, and my Self,
There, freed of myself,
In a stricken shade dancing together,
As a wave rolled under the water,

Lifted and rose in our images
The king wears newly, redoubling.

Where we went in, all power failed the house.
I spooned out light
Upon a candle thread. My wife lay down.
Through the flaming, white-bread nerve
I peered from the eye of the mind.
No child from the windowed dark came forth
To the hand, in its pure-blooded fire,
But the basket glow of the crown.
The glass fetched white to a breath; I understood
How the crown must come from within:
Of water made, and a wheel,
And of the thing in flame that seems to pant.
In a movement you cannot imagine
Of mirrors, the gulls fall, hidden.

I lay in bed. One hand in its sleeve
Lay open, on my breath.
My shadow, struck down beneath me,
Rose, through my form. I heard the bell,
In mist, step backwardly onto the waves.
The wind fell off, as candle shade
Unraveled our walls like knitting, and I,
Undone, outstretched through the trampled shining
Of thousands of miles of the moon,
And the fallen king
Breathed like a nosebleed, there,
Two men wear newly, in hiding.
In a movement you cannot imagine
Of bloodshed, the gulls fall, inward.

I listened for the coming of a barge.
In a cat's-cradling motion
Of oars, my father rocked, in the mist. He died;
He was dying. His whisper fell,
As I, beneath the grave. Below the drowned

I panted, in the pig-iron taste of my beard.
I yelled, as out of a bucket,
Through my fettered mask, before the dawn
When my arms, my big-footed legs would hang
From pothooks, strange and untimely.
The stone beat like a gull; my father's voice
Came to life, in words, in my ear.
In a movement you cannot imagine
Of prison, the gulls turn, calling.

Believing, then, astoundedly, in a son,
I drew from tufted stone
My sword. I slew my murderer, Lightborn, on the stair:
With the flat of steel, I flashed
Him dead, through his eyes high-piled in the hood.
When the tide came in, I rose
And onto the curded dark climbed out.
In the cliffs, where creatures about me swam,
In their thin, slain, time-serving bones,
The heavy page, the animal print of the chalk,
With wounds I glittered, dazzling as a fish.
In my short-horned, wool-gathering crown
I came from the beasts to the kingdoms
The king wears newly, in passing.

The sun fell down, through the moon.
The dead held house.
I hove my father to my back
And climbed from his barrow, there.
Pride helped me pick a queen and get a son.
The heroic drink of the womb
Broke, then, into swanlike song.
One came with scepter, one with cup,
On goatlike back'd, and one with the head of a god.
My mask fell away, and my gyves.
Through my sons I leapt in my ghost
The king wears newly, on fire.
In a movement you cannot imagine
Of birth, the gulls fall, crying.

In the cloudlike, packed, and layered realm
I wept, when I would sing.
I laid my father down where he must lie,
And entered, again, in my passion,
An older, incredible shape
Becoming young, as the cliffs let fall within stone
Their shadow green down from the crest.
I stood on the cliff top, alone.
My father's body in my heart
Like a buried candle danced. I saw it shed on the sea,
On the flats of water, far out:
A rough, selected brightness
Exchanging a flame for a wheel
The king wears slowly, in measure.

Birds drifted in my breath as it was drawn
From the stressing glitter
Of water. Where France becomes
Another blue lid for the eye,
I felt my green eyes turn
Surpassingly blue, of one great look upon distance.
The sword dissolved, in my hands; wings beat.
I watched them rise from my arms, and stood
Excited forever by love. I saw the child's eye shine
From his book, a wave of justified light.
The prisons like organs moaned. In a death like life
I sang like a head on a pole.
In a movement you cannot imagine
Of emblems, the gulls fall, silent.

One foot shone to me, from the sun.
I felt the sun's
Mortality increase. In the blown,
Brow-beating light, I woke, and saw the room
Arise like a yeast from the floor,
The window come down like a bee.
In the long-legged, warm-bodied bed
I thought of him who would tell

To himself, arising in candle-cast bones:
Every man, every man
Not a king. It is I
The king wears newly, in lasting.
In a movement you cannot imagine
Of spells, the gulls fall, listening.

How shall the stranger wake
Who has issued from dark
With the king? With gulls asleep
In the blue-burning grass? And on the sea,
A blaze that is counting itself,
The white birds holding
Still, on the field of the cloth of gold,
On the self and soul of the air?
Who stands, big-footed with glory, yet,
With the sound falling out of his voice
And his voice halfway to his son
Whose breath Time holds, in a woman?
In a movement you cannot imagine
Of silence, the gulls fall, waiting.

Why not as a prince, who, as
From a distance, wakes?
Who turns from the regular mirror
To watch, at the flawing pane,
Pale fire on a hairspring still burning
In the puddled socket, and the fishing flash
On the shuffled rock of a wave
Overturn, an inlaid crash
In the window's half-mirror, half-air
As he steps through this room from the sea?
A tossed, green crown on his head,
He combs down the hair of his spirit,
Which is dead, but for the eyes
The king wears newly, at thirty:

Yet who is *he?* Whom does he face, in reflection?
The stained-glass king,
Or the child, grown tall, who cried to earth and air,
To books and water: to sun and father and fire
And nothingness to come and crown him, here?
Or are they, both of them, and neither,
This straw-headed knave, in blue-printed blue jeans appearing:
Who, in exultant tenderness upon a woman's sleep
Onlooks, then leaps out the door, out of that
Up onto the seaside path, and when the sheep track dies,
Two late and idle lovers in the grass
Kicks into love, and goes up the cliffs to be crowned?
In a movement you cannot imagine
Of England, the king smiles, climbing: running.

TO HIS CHILDREN IN DARKNESS

You hear my step
Come close, and stop.
I shut the door.
By the two-deck bed
And its breathing sheets
Houselight is killed
From off my breast.
I am unseen,
But sensed, but known,
And now begin

To be what I
Can never be,
But what I am
Within your dream:
A god or beast
Come true at last.
To one, I have
Like leaves grown here,
And furl my wings
As poplars sigh,

And slowly let
On him a breath
Drawn in a cloud,
In which he sees
Angelic hosts
Like blowing trees
Send me to earth
To root among
The secret soil
Of his dark room.

The other hears
A creature shed
Throughout the maze
The same long breath
As he conceives

That he no more
Desires to live
In blazing sun,
Nor shake to death
The animal

Of his own head.
I know what lies
Behind all words,
Like a beast, mismade,
Which finds its brain
Can sing alone
Without a sound
At what he is
And cannot change,
Or like a god

Which slowly breathes
Eternal life
Upon a soul
In deepest sleep.
My heart's one move
Comes now, and now.
A god strikes root
On touching earth.
A beast can hold
The thought of self

Between his horns
Until it shines.
That you may feel
What I must be
And cannot know
By standing here,
My sons, I bring
These beings home
Into your room.
They are. I am.

A SCREENED PORCH IN THE COUNTRY

All of them are sitting
Inside a lamp of coarse wire
And being in all directions
Shed upon darkness,
Their bodies softening to shadow, until
They come to rest out in the yard
In a kind of blurred golden country
In which they more deeply lie
Than if they were being created
Of Heavenly light.

Where they are floating beyond
Themselves, in peace,
Where they have laid down
Their souls and not known it,
The smallest creatures,
As every night they do,
Come to the edge of them
And sing, if they can,
Or, if they can't, simply shine
Their eyes back, sitting on haunches,

Pulsating and thinking of music.
Occasionally, something weightless
Touches the screen
With its body, dies,
Or is unmurmuringly hurt,
But mainly nothing happens
Except that a family continues
To be laid down
In the midst of its nightly creatures,
Not one of which openly comes

Into the golden shadow
Where the people are lying,
Emitted by their own house
So humanly that they become
More than human, and enter the place

Of small, blindly singing things,
Seeming to rejoice
Perpetually, without effort,
Without knowing why
Or how they do it.

HUNTING CIVIL WAR RELICS AT NIMBLEWILL CREEK

As he moves the mine detector
A few inches over the ground,
Making it vitally float
Among the ferns and weeds,
I come into this war
Slowly, with my one brother,
Watching his face grow deep
Between the earphones,
For I can tell
If we enter the buried battle
Of Nimblewill
Only by his expression.

Softly he wanders, parting
The grass with a dreaming hand.
No dead cry yet takes root
In his clapped ears
Or can be seen in his smile.
But underfoot I feel
The dead regroup,
The burst metals all in place,
The battle lines be drawn
Anew to include us
In Nimblewill,
And I carry the shovel and pick

More as if they were
Bright weapons that I bore.
A bird's cry breaks
In two, and into three parts.
We cross the creek; the cry
Shifts into another,
Nearer, bird, and is
Like the shout of a shadow—
Lived-with, appallingly close—
Or the soul, pronouncing
"Nimblewill":
Three tones; your being changes.

We climb the bank;
A faint light glows
On my brother's mouth.
I listen, as two birds fight
For a single voice, but he
Must be hearing the grave,
In pieces, all singing
To his clamped head,
For he smiles as if
He rose from the dead within
Green Nimblewill
And stood in his grandson's shape.

No shot from the buried war
Shall kill me now,
For the dead have waited here
A hundred years to create
Only the look on the face
Of my one brother,
Who stands among them, offering
A metal dish
Afloat in the trembling weeds,
With a long-buried light on his lips
At Nimblewill
And the dead outsinging two birds.

I choke the handle
Of the pick, and fall to my knees
To dig wherever he points,
To bring up mess tin or bullet,
To go underground
Still singing, myself,
Without a sound,
Like a man who renounces war,
Or one who shall lift up the past,
Not breathing "Father,"
At Nimblewill,
But saying, "Fathers! Fathers!"

THE HOSPITAL WINDOW

I have just come down from my father.
Higher and higher he lies
Above me in a blue light
Shed by a tinted window.
I drop through six white floors
And then step out onto pavement.

Still feeling my father ascend,
I start to cross the firm street,
My shoulder blades shining with all
The glass the huge building can raise.
Now I must turn round and face it,
And know his one pane from the others.

Each window possesses the sun
As though it burned there on a wick.
I wave, like a man catching fire.
All the deep-dyed windowpanes flash,
And, behind them, all the white rooms
They turn to the color of Heaven.

Ceremoniously, gravely, and weakly,
Dozens of pale hands are waving
Back, from inside their flames.
Yet one pure pane among these
Is the bright, erased blankness of nothing.
I know that my father is there,

In the shape of his death still living.
The traffic increases around me
Like a madness called down on my head.
The horns blast at me like shotguns,
And drivers lean out, driven crazy—
But now my propped-up father

Lifts his arm out of stillness at last.
The light from the window strikes me
And I turn as blue as a soul,

As the moment when I was born.
I am not afraid for my father—
Look! He is grinning; he is not

Afraid for my life, either,
As the wild engines stand at my knees
Shredding their gears and roaring,
And I hold each car in its place
For miles, inciting its horn
To blow down the walls of the world

That the dying may float without fear
In the bold blue gaze of my father.
Slowly I move to the sidewalk
With my pin-tingling hand half dead
At the end of my bloodless arm.
I carry it off in amazement,

High, still higher, still waving,
My recognized face fully mortal,
Yet not; not at all, in the pale,
Drained, otherworldly, stricken,
Created hue of stained glass.
I have just come down from my father.

IV

THE MAGUS

It is time for the others to come.
This child is no more than a god.

No cars are moving this night.
The lights in the houses go out.

I put these out with the rest.
From his crib, the child begins

To shine, letting forth one ray
Through the twelve simple bars of his bed

Down into the trees, where two
Long-lost other men shall be drawn

Slowly up to the brink of the house,
Slowly in through the breath on the window.

But how did I get in this room?
Is this my son, or another's?

Where is the woman to tell me
How my face is lit up by his body?

It is time for the others to come.
An event more miraculous yet

Is the thing I am shining to tell you.
This child is no more than a child.

These are stone jetties,
And, in the close part of the night,
Connected to my feet by long
Warm, dangling shadows
On the buttressed water,
Boats are at rest.

Beyond, the harbor mouth opens
Much as you might believe
A human mouth would open
To say that all things are a darkness.
I sit believing this
As the boats beneath me dissolve

And shake with a haunted effort
To come into being again,
And my son nods at my side,
Looking out also
Into dark, through the painted
Living shadows of dead-still hulls

Toward where we imagine Africa
To bloom late at night
Like a lamp of sand held up,
A top-heavy hourglass, perhaps,
With its heaped, eternal grains
Falling, falling

Into the lower, green part
Which gives off quick, leafy flashes
Like glimpses of lightning.
We strain to encounter that image
Halfway from its shore to ours:
To understand

The undermined glowing of sand
Lifted at midnight
Somewhere far out above water,

The effortless flicker of trees
Where a rumor of beasts moves slowly
Like wave upon wave.

What life have we entered by this?
Here, where our bodies are,
With a green and gold light on his face,
My staring child's hand is in mine,
And in the stone
Fear like a dancing of peoples.

Dark, deeply. A red.
All levels moving
A given surface.
Break this. Step down.
Follow your right
Foot nakedly in
To another body.
Put on the river
Like a fleeing coat,
A garment of motion,
Tremendous, immortal.
Find a still root

To hold you in it.
Let flowing create
A new, inner being:
As the source in the mountain
Gives water in pulses,
These can be felt at
The heart of the current.
And here it is only
One wandering step
Forth, to the sea.
Your freed hair floating
Out of your brain,

Wait for a coming
And swimming idea.
Live like the dead
In their flying feeling.
Loom as a ghost
When life pours through it.
Crouch in the secret
Released underground
With the earth of the fields
All around you, gone
Into purposeful grains
That stream like dust

In a holy hallway.
Weight more changed
Than that of one
Now being born,
Let go the root.
Move with the world
As the deep dead move,
Opposed to nothing.
Release. Enter the sea
Like a winding wind.
No. Rise. Draw breath.
Sing. See no one.

THE SALT MARSH

Once you have let the first blade
Spring back behind you
To the way it has always been,
You no longer know where you are.
All you can see are the tall
Stalks of sawgrass, not sawing,
But each of them holding its tip
Exactly at the level where your hair

Begins to grow from your forehead.
Wherever you come to is
The same as before,
With the same blades of oversized grass,
And wherever you stop, the one
Blade just in front of you leans,
That one only, and touches you
At the place where your hair begins

To grow; at that predestined touch
Your spine tingles crystally, like salt,
And the image of a crane occurs,
Each flap of its wings creating
Its feathers anew, this time whiter,
As the sun destroys all points
Of the compass, refusing to move
From its chosen noon.

Where is the place you have come from
With your buried steps full of new roots?
You cannot leap up to look out,
Yet you do not sink,
But seem to grow, and the sound,
The oldest of sounds, is your breath
Sighing like acres.
If you stand as you are for long,

Green panic may finally give
Way to another sensation,
For when the embodying wind
Rises, the grasses begin to weave
A little, then all together,
Not bending enough for you
To see your way clear of the swaying,
But moving just the same,

And nothing prevents your bending
With them, helping their wave
Upon wave upon wave upon wave
By not opposing,
By willing your supple inclusion
Among fields without promise of harvest,
In their marvelous, spiritual walking
Everywhere, anywhere.

I am hearing the shape of the rain
Take the shape of the tent and believe it,
Laying down all around where I lie
A profound, unspeakable law.
I obey, and am free-falling slowly

Through the thought-out leaves of the wood
Into the minds of animals.
I am there in the shining of water
Like dark, like light, out of Heaven.

I am there like the dead, or the beast
Itself, which thinks of a poem—
Green, plausible, living, and holy—
And cannot speak, but hears,
Called forth from the waiting of things,

A vast, proper, reinforced crying
With the sifted, harmonious pause,
The sustained intake of all breath
Before the first word of the Bible.

At midnight water dawns
Upon the held skulls of the foxes
And weasels and tousled hares
On the eastern side of the mountain.
Their light is the image I make

As I wait as if recently killed,
Receptive, fragile, half-smiling,
My brow watermarked with the mark
On the wing of a moth

And the tent taking shape on my body
Like ill-fitting, Heavenly clothes.

From holes in the ground comes my voice
In the God-silenced tongue of the beasts.
"I shall rise from the dead," I am saying.

Helmets

To Maxine
light and warmth

I

THE DUSK OF HORSES

Right under their noses, the green
Of the field is paling away
Because of something fallen from the sky.

They see this, and put down
Their long heads deeper in grass
That only just escapes reflecting them

As the dream of a millpond would.
The color green flees over the grass
Like an insect, following the red sun over

The next hill. The grass is white.
There is no cloud so dark and white at once;
There is no pool at dawn that deepens

Their faces and thirsts as this does.
Now they are feeding on solid
Cloud, and, one by one,

With nails as silent as stars among the wood
Hewed down years ago and now rotten,
The stalls are put up around them.

Now if they lean, they come
On wood on any side. Not touching it, they sleep.
No beast ever lived who understood

What happened among the sun's fields,
Or cared why the color of grass
Fled over the hill while he stumbled,

Led by the halter to sleep
On his four taxed, worthy legs.
Each thinks he awakens where

The sun is black on the rooftop,
That the green is dancing in the next pasture,
And that the way to sleep

In a cloud, or in a risen lake,
Is to walk as though he were still
In the drained field standing, head down,

To pretend to sleep when led,
And thus to go under the ancient white
Of the meadow, as green goes

And whiteness comes up through his face
Holding stars and rotten rafters,
Quiet, fragrant, and relieved.

Too tight, it is running over
Too much of this ground to be still
Or to do anything but tremble
And disappear left and right
As far as the eye can see

Over hills, through woods,
Down roads, to arrive at last
Again where it connects,
Coming back from the other side
Of animals, defining their earthly estate

As the grass becomes snow
While they are standing and dreaming
Of grass and snow.
The winter hawk that sits upon its post,
Feeling the airy current of the wires,

Turns into a robin, sees that this is wrong,
Then into a boy, and into a man who holds
His palm on the top tense strand
With the whole farm feeding slowly
And nervously into his hand.

If the wire were cut anywhere
All his blood would fall to the ground
And leave him standing and staring
With a face as white as a Hereford's.
From years of surrounding grain,

Cows, horses, machinery trying to turn
To rust, the humming arrives each second,
A sound that arranges these acres
And holds them highstrung and enthralled.
Because of the light, chilled hand

On the top thread tuned to an E
Like the low string of a guitar,

The dead corn is more
Balanced in death than it was,
The animals more aware

Within the huge human embrace
Held up and borne out of sight
Upon short, unbreakable poles
Wherethrough the ruled land intones
Like a psalm: properly,

With its eyes closed,
Whether on the side of the animals
Or not, whether disappearing
Right, left, through trees or down roads,
Whether outside, around, or in.

The sea here used to look
As if many convicts had built it,

Standing deep in their ankle chains,
Ankle-deep in the water, to smite

The land and break it down to salt.
I was in this bog as a child

When they were all working all day
To drive the pilings down.

I thought I saw the still sun
Strike the side of a hammer in flight

And from it a sea bird be born
To take off over the marshes.

As the gray climbs the side of my head
And cuts my brain off from the world,

I walk and wish mainly for birds,
For the one bird no one has looked for

To spring again from a flash
Of metal, perhaps from the scratched

Wedding band on my ring finger.
Recalling the chains of their feet,

I stand and look out over grasses
At the bridge they built, long abandoned,

Breaking down into water at last,
And long, like them, for freedom

Or death, or to believe again
That they worked on the ocean to give it

The unchanging, hopeless look
Out of which all miracles leap.

There are two facing peacocks
    Or a ship flapping
On its own white tufted sail
At roadside, near a mill;

Flamingoes also are hanging
    By their bills on bedspreads
And an occasional mallard.
These you can buy anywhere.
They are made by machine
From a sanctioned, unholy pattern
Rigid with industry.
They hoard the smell of oil

And hum like looms all night
    Into your pores, reweaving
Your body from bobbins.
There is only one quiet

Place—in a scuppernong arbor—
    Where animals as they
Would be, are born into sleep-cloth:
A middle-aged man's grandmother
Sits in the summer green light
Of leaves, gone toothless
For eating grapes better,
And pulls the animals through

With a darning needle:
    Deer, rabbits and birds,
Red whales and unicorns,
Winged elephants, crowned ants:

Beasts that cannot be thought of
    By the wholly sane
Rise up in the rough, blurred
Flowers of fuzzy cloth
In only their timeless outlines

Like the beasts of Heaven:
Those sketched out badly, divinely
By stars not wholly sane.

Love, I have slept in that house.
          There it was winter.
The tattered moonfields crept
Through the trellis, and fell

In vine-tangled shade on my face
          Like thrown-away knitting
Before cloud came and dimmed
Those scars from off me.
My fingernails chilled
To the bone. I called
For another body to be
With me, and warm us both.

A unicorn neighed; I folded
          His neck in my arms
And was safe, as he lay down.
All night, from thickening Heaven,

Someone up there kept throwing
          Bedspreads upon me.
Softly I called, and they came:
The ox and the basilisk,

The griffin, the phoenix, the lion—
Light-bodied, only the essence,
The tufted, creative starfields
Behind the assembling clouds—

The snake from the apple tree came
          To save me from freezing,
And at last the lung-winged ship
On its own sail scented with potash

Fell sighing upon us all.
The last two nails
Of cold died out in my nostrils
Under the dance-weight of beasts.
I lay, breathing like thread,
An inspired outline of myself,
As rain began greatly to fall,
And closed the door of the Ark.

ON THE COOSAWATTEE

1. By Canoe Through the Fir Forest

Into the slain tons of needles,
On something like time and dark knowledge
That cannot be told, we are riding
Over white stones forward through fir trees,
To follow whatever the river
Through the clasping of roots follows deeply.

As we go inward, more trunks
Climb from the edge of the water
And turn on the banks and stand growing.
The nerves in the patches of tree-light
On the ripples can feel no death,
But shake like the wings of angels

With light hard-pressed to keep up
Though it is in place on each feather.
Heavy woods in one movement around us
Flow back along either side
Bringing in more essential curves;
Small stones in their thousands turn corners

Under water and bear us on
Through the glittering, surfacing wingbeats
Cast from above. As we pass over,
As we pass through each hover of gold,
We lift up our blades from the water
And the blades of our shoulders,

Our rowing-muscles, our wings,
Are still and tremble, undying,
Drifting deeper into the forest.
Each light comes into our life
Past the man in front's changed hair
Then along the wing-balancing floor

And then onto me and one eye
And into my mouth for an instant.

The stones beneath us grow rounder
As I taste the fretted light fall
Through living needles to be here
Like a word I can feed on forever

Or believe like a vision I have
Or want to conceive out of greenness.
While the world fades, it is *becoming*.
As the trees shut away all seeing,
In my mouth I mix it with sunlight.
Here, in the dark, it is *being*.

    II. *Below Ellijay*
Coming into Ellijay on the green
Idling freeway of the broad river
From the hill farms and pine woods,
We saw first the little stores
That backed down the red clay banks,
The blue flash of bottleglass
And the rippled tin heat haze of sheds

Where country mechanics were frying.
A poultry-processing plant
Smoked in the late morning air;
The bridge we rode under clattered
As we wound back out into fields.
But the water that held us had changed;
The town had slowed it and used it;

The wind had died in the tool sheds.
When we looked overboard, we knew.
Each thing was mistakenly feathered,
Muffled thickly in cast-off whiteness:
Each log was bedraggled in plumage
And accepting more feathers from water;
Each boulder under the green

Was becoming a lewd, setting hen
Moultingly under us brooding
In the sick, buried wind of the river,

Wavering, dying, increasing
From the plucked refuse of the plant,
And beside us uselessly floated —
Following, dipping, returning,

Turning frankly around to eye us,
To eye something else, to eye
Us again—a skinned chicken head,
Its gaze unperturbed and abiding.
All morning we floated on feathers
Among the drawn heads which appeared
Everywhere, from under the logs

Of feathers, from upstream behind us,
Lounging back to us from ahead,
Until we believed ourselves doomed
And the planet corrupted forever,
With stones turned to pullets, not struggling
But into more monstrousness shed,
Our canoe trailing more and more feathers

And the eye of the devil upon us
Closing drunkenly in from all sides,
And could have been on the Styx
In the blaze of noon, till we felt
The quickening pulse of the rapids
And entered upon it like men
Who sense that the world can be cleansed

Among rocks pallid only with water,
And plunged there like the unborn
Who see earthly streams without taint
Flow beneath them, while their wing feathers
Slough off behind them in Heaven
As they dress in the blinding clothes
Of nakedness for their fall.

III. *The Inundation*
Down there is a stone that holds my deepest sleep
And buries it deeper and deeper

Under the green, skinny lake
That is going back into the Georgia hills
And climbing them day and night
Behind the new dam.

And there is another stone, that boiled with white,
Where Braselton and I clung and fought
With our own canoe
That flung us in the rapids we had ridden
So that it might turn and take on
A ton of mountain water

And swing and bear down through the flying cloud
Of foam upon our violent rock
And pin us there.
With our backs to the wall of that boulder,
We yelled and kept it off us as we could,
Broke both paddles,

Then wedged it with the paddle stumps up over
The rock till the hull split, and it leapt and fell
Into the afterfall.
In life preservers we whirled ourselves away
And floated aimlessly down into calm water,
Turning like objects,

Then crawled upon shore and were found in the afternoon
By Lucas Gentry and his hunting dog, asleep
On a vast, gentle stone.
At a touch we woke, and followed the strange woods boy
Up the bluff, looking down on the roaring river's
Last day in its bed.

And now I cannot sleep at all, until I think
Of the Coosa, out of a clear blue sky
Overswelling its banks,
Its great stones falling through it into dark,
Its creeks becoming inlets, where water
Skiers already poise.

Over me it rises, too, but breathable, like cloud,
A green and silver cloud above which quiet
Lucas Gentry stands.
His dog whines, as the last rock of the wild river
Goes under, its white water lapses green,
And the leaping stone

Where we almost died takes on the settled repose
Of that other where we lay down and met
Our profoundest sleep
Rising from it to us, as the battered sides
Of the canoe gave deeper and deeper shade,
And Lucas Gentry,

Who may have been the accepting spirit of the place
Come to call us to higher ground,
Bent to raise
Us from the sleep of the yet-to-be-drowned,
There, with the black dream of the dead canoe
Over our faces.

WINTER TROUT

In the concrete cells of the hatchery
He nourished a dream of living
Under the ice, the long preparations
For the strange heat of feeling slowly

Roofs melt to a rhythmic green,
But now, in the first cold of freedom,
Riding motionless under the road
Of ice, shaping the heart

Of the buried stream with his tail,
He knows that his powers come
From the fire and stillness of freezing.
With the small tremors of his form

The banks shift imperceptibly,
Shift back, tremble, settle,
Shift, all within utter stillness.
I keep in my quiver now

An arrow whose head is half-missing.
It is useless, but I will not change
The pulled, broken tooth of its head
For I have walked upon banks

Shaken with the watchfulness of trout
Like walking barefoot in sleep
On the swaying tips of a grainfield,
On the long, just-bending stems,

Almost weightless, able to leap
Great distances, yet not leaping
Because each step on that ground
Gave a new sense of limitless hope.

Under the ice the trout rode,
Trembling, in the mastered heart

Of the creek, with what he could do.
I set myself up as a statue

With a bow, my red woolen back
Climbed slowly by thoughtful brambles
And dead beggar-lice, to shoot
At an angle down through the shadow

Of ice, and spear the trout
With a shot like Ulysses'
Through the ax heads, with the great weapon.
I shot, and the trout did not move

But was gone, and the banks
Went rigid under my feet
As the arrow floated away
Under the paving of ice.

I froze my right hand to retrieve it
As a blessing or warning,
As a sign of the penalties
For breaking into closed worlds

Where the wary controllers lie
At the heart of their power,
A pure void of shadowy purpose
Where the gods live, attuning the world,

Laying plans for the first green
They ever have lived, to melt
The ice from their great crowns.
Their secret enemies break

Like statues, as the king rises slowly,
Keeping only the thinnest film
Of his element—imagination—
Before his eyes as he lifts

Into spring, with the wood upside down
Balanced perfectly in all its leaves

And roots as he deeply has
All winter made provision for,

The surface full of gold flakes
Of the raw undersides of leaves,
And the thing seen right,
For once, that winter bought.

SPRINGER MOUNTAIN

Four sweaters are woven upon me,
All black, all sweating and waiting,
And a sheepherder's coat's wool hood,
Buttoned strainingly, holds my eyes
With their sight deepfrozen outside them
From their gaze toward a single tree.
I am here where I never have been,
In the limbs of my warmest clothes,
Waiting for light to crawl, weakly
From leaf to dead leaf onto leaf
Down the western side of the mountain.
Deer sleeping in light far above me

Have already woken, and moved,
In step with the sun moving strangely
Down toward the dark knit of my thicket
Where my breath takes shape on the air
Like a white helmet come from the lungs.
The one tree I hope for goes inward
And reaches the limbs of its gold.
My eyesight hangs partly between
Two twigs on the upslanting ground,
Then steps like a god from the dead
Wet of a half-rotted oak log
Steeply into the full of my brow.
My thighbones groaningly break

Upward, releasing my body
To climb, and to find among humus
New insteps made of snapped sticks.
On my back the faggot of arrows
Rattles and scratches its feathers.

I go up over logs slowly
On my painfully reborn legs,
My ears putting out vast hearing
Among the invisible animals,

Passing under thin branches held still,
Kept formed all night as they were
By the thought of predictable light.
The sun comes openly in
To my mouth, and is blown out white,

But no deer is anywhere near me.
I sit down and wait as in darkness.

The sweat goes dead at the roots

Of my hair: a deer is created
Descending, then standing and looking.
The sun stands and waits for his horns

To move. I may be there, also,
Between them, in head bones uplifted
Like a man in an animal tree
Nailed until light comes:
A dream of the unfeared hunter
Who has formed in his brain in the dark
And rose with light into his horns,
Naked, and I have turned younger

At forty than I ever have been.
I hang my longbow on a branch.
The buck leaps away and then stops,
And I step forward, stepping out

Of my shadow and pulling over
My head one dark heavy sweater
After another, my dungarees falling
Till they can be kicked away,
Boots, socks, all that is on me
Off. The world catches fire.
I put an unbearable light
Into breath skinned alive of its garments:
I think, beginning with laurel,

Like a beast loving
With the whole god bone of his horns:
The green of excess is upon me
Like deer in fir thickets in winter
Stamping and dreaming of men
Who will kneel with them naked to break
The ice from streams with their faces
And drink from the lifespring of beasts.
He is moving. I am with him

Down the shuddering hillside moving
Through trees and around, inside
And out of stumps and groves
Of laurel and slash pine,
Through hip-searing branches and thorn
Brakes, unprotected and sure,
Winding down to the waters of life
Where they stand petrified in a creek bed
Yet melt and flow from the hills
At the touch of an animal visage,

Rejoicing wherever I come to
With the gold of my breast unwrapped,
My crazed laughter pure as good church-cloth,
My brain dazed and pointed with trying
To grow horns, glad that it cannot,
For a few steps deep in the dance
Of what I most am and should be
And can be only once in this life.
He is gone below, and I limp
To look for my clothes in the world,

A middle-aged, softening man
Grinning and shaking his head
In amazement to last him forever.
I put on the warm-bodied wool,
The four sweaters inside out,
The bootlaces dangling and tripping,

Then pick my tense bow off the limb
And turn with the unwinding hooftracks,
In my good, tricked clothes,
To hunt, under Springer Mountain,
Deer for the first and last time.

II

CHERRYLOG ROAD

Off Highway 106
At Cherrylog Road I entered
The '34 Ford without wheels,
Smothered in kudzu,
With a seat pulled out to run
Corn whiskey down from the hills,

And then from the other side
Crept into an Essex
With a rumble seat of red leather
And then out again, aboard
A blue Chevrolet, releasing
The rust from its other color,

Reared up on three building blocks.
None had the same body heat;
I changed with them inward, toward
The weedy heart of the junkyard,
For I knew that Doris Holbrook
Would escape from her father at noon

And would come from the farm
To seek parts owned by the sun
Among the abandoned chassis,
Sitting in each in turn
As I did, leaning forward
As in a wild stock-car race

In the parking lot of the dead.
Time after time, I climbed in
And out the other side, like
An envoy or movie star
Met at the station by crickets.
A radiator cap raised its head,

Become a real toad or a kingsnake
As I neared the hub of the yard,
Passing through many states,
Many lives, to reach
Some grandmother's long Pierce-Arrow
Sending platters of blindness forth

From its nickel hubcaps
And spilling its tender upholstery
On sleepy roaches,
The glass panel in between
Lady and colored driver
Not all the way broken out,

The back-seat phone
Still on its hook.
I got in as though to exclaim,
"Let us go to the orphan asylum,
John; I have some old toys
For children who say their prayers."

I popped with sweat as I thought
I heard Doris Holbrook scrape
Like a mouse in the southern-state sun
That was eating the paint in blisters
From a hundred car tops and hoods.
She was tapping like code,

Loosening the screws,
Carrying off headlights,
Sparkplugs, bumpers,
Cracked mirrors and gear-knobs,
Getting ready, already,
To go back with something to show

Other than her lips' new trembling
I would hold to me soon, soon,
Where I sat in the ripped back seat
Talking over the interphone,

Praying for Doris Holbrook
To come from her father's farm

And to get back there
With no trace of me on her face
To be seen by her red-haired father
Who would change, in the squalling barn,
Her back's pale skin with a strop,
Then lay for me

In a bootlegger's roasting car
With a string-triggered 12-gauge shotgun
To blast the breath from the air.
Not cut by the jagged windshields,
Through the acres of wrecks she came
With a wrench in her hand,

Through dust where the blacksnake dies
Of boredom, and the beetle knows
The compost has no more life.
Someone outside would have seen
The oldest car's door inexplicably
Close from within:

I held her and held her and held her,
Convoyed at terrific speed
By the stalled, dreaming traffic around us,
So the blacksnake, stiff
With inaction, curved back
Into life, and hunted the mouse

With deadly overexcitement,
The beetles reclaimed their field
As we clung, glued together,
With the hooks of the seat springs
Working through to catch us red-handed
Amidst the gray breathless batting

That burst from the seat at our backs.
We left by separate doors

Into the changed, other bodies
Of cars, she down Cherrylog Road
And I to my motorcycle
Parked like the soul of the junkyard

Restored, a bicycle fleshed
With power, and tore off
Up Highway 106, continually
Drunk on the wind in my mouth,
Wringing the handlebar for speed,
Wild to be wreckage forever.

THE SCARRED GIRL

All glass may yet be whole
She thinks, it may be put together
From the deep inner flashing of her face.
One moment the windshield held

The countryside, the green
Level fields and the animals,
And these must be restored
To what they were when her brow

Broke into them for nothing, and began
Its sparkling under the gauze.
Though the still, small war for her beauty
Is stitched out of sight and lost,

It is not this field that she thinks of.
It is that her face, buried
And held up inside the slow scars,
Knows how the bright, fractured world

Burns and pulls and weeps
To come together again.
The green meadow lying in fragments
Under the splintered sunlight,

The cattle broken in pieces
By her useless, painful intrusion
Know that her visage contains
The process and hurt of their healing,

The hidden wounds that can
Restore anything, bringing the glass
Of the world together once more,
All as it was when she struck,

All except her. The shattered field
Where they dragged the telescoped car

Off to be pounded to scrap
Waits for her to get up,

For her calm, unimagined face
To emerge from the yards of its wrapping,
Red, raw, mixed-looking but entire,
A new face, an old life,

To confront the pale glass it has dreamed
Made whole and backed with wise silver,
Held in other hands brittle with dread,
A doctor's, a lip-biting nurse's,

Who do not see what she sees
Behind her odd face in the mirror:
The pastures of earth and of heaven
Restored and undamaged, the cattle

Risen out of their jagged graves
To walk in the seamless sunlight
And a newborn countenance
Put upon everything,

Her beauty gone, but to hover
Near for the rest of her life,
And good no nearer, but plainly
In sight, and the only way.

KUDZU

Japan invades. Far Eastern vines
Run from the clay banks they are

Supposed to keep from eroding,
Up telephone poles,
Which rear, half out of leafage,
As though they would shriek,
Like things smothered by their own
Green, mindless, unkillable ghosts.
In Georgia, the legend says
That you must close your windows

At night to keep it out of the house.
The glass is tinged with green, even so,

As the tendrils crawl over the fields.
The night the kudzu has
Your pasture, you sleep like the dead.
Silence has grown Oriental
And you cannot step upon ground:
Your leg plunges somewhere
It should not, it never should be,
Disappears, and waits to be struck

Anywhere between sole and kneecap:
For when the kudzu comes,

The snakes do, and weave themselves
Among its lengthening vines,
Their spade heads resting on leaves,
Growing also, in earthly power
And the huge circumstance of concealment.
One by one the cows stumble in,
Drooling a hot green froth,
And die, seeing the wood of their stalls

Strain to break into leaf.
In your closed house, with the vine

Tapping your window like lightning,
You remember what tactics to use.
In the wrong yellow fog-light of dawn
You herd them in, the hogs,
Head down in their hairy fat,
The meaty troops, to the pasture.
The leaves of the kudzu quake
With the serpents' fear, inside

The meadow ringed with men
Holding sticks, on the country roads.

The hogs disappear in the leaves.
The sound is intense, subhuman,
Nearly human with purposive rage.
There is no terror
Sound from the snakes.
No one can see the desperate, futile
Striking under the leaf heads.
Now and then, the flash of a long

Living vine, a cold belly,
Leaps up, torn apart, then falls
Under the tussling surface.
You have won, and wait for frost,
When, at the merest touch
Of cold, the kudzu turns
Black, withers inward and dies,
Leaving a mass of brown strings
Like the wires of a gigantic switchboard.
You open your windows,

With the lightning restored to the sky
And no leaves rising to bury

You alive inside your frail house,
And you think, in the opened cold,
Of the surface of things and its terrors,
And of the mistaken, mortal
Arrogance of the snakes

As the vines, growing insanely, sent
Great powers into their bodies
And the freedom to strike without warning:

From them, though they killed
Your cattle, such energy also flowed

To you from the knee-high meadow
(It was as though you had
A green sword twined among
The veins of your growing right arm—
Such strength as you would not believe
If you stood alone in a proper
Shaved field among your safe cows—):
Came in through your closed

Leafy windows and almighty sleep
And prospered, till rooted out.

Far away under us, they are mowing on the green steps
Of the valley, taking long, unending swings
Among the ripe wheat.
It is something about them growing,
Growing smaller, that makes us look up and see
That what has come over them is a storm.

It is a blue-black storm the shape of this valley,
And includes, perhaps, in its darkness,
Three men in the air
Taking long, limber swings, cutting water.
Swaths start to fall and, on earth,
The men come closer together as they mow.

Now in the last stand of wheat they bend.
From above, we watch over them like gods,
Our chins on our hands,
Our great eyes staring, our throats dry
And aching to cry down on their heads
Some curse or blessing,

Some word we have never known, but we feel
That when the right time arrives, and more stillness,
Lightning will leap
From our mouths in reasonless justice
As they arc their scythes more slowly, taking care
Not to look up.

As darkness increases there comes
A dancing into each of their swings,
A dancing like men in a cloud.
We two are coming together
Also, along the wall.
No lightning yet falls from us

Where their long hooks catch on the last of the sun
And the color of the wheat passes upward,
Drawn off like standing water

Into the cloud, turning green;
The field becomes whiter and darker,
And fire in us gathers and gathers

Not to call down death to touch brightly
The only metal for miles
In the hands of judged, innocent men,
But for our use only, who in the first sheaves of rain
Sit thunderstruck, having now the power to speak
With deadly intent of love.

THE POISONED MAN

When the rattlesnake bit, I lay
In a dream of the country, and dreamed
Day after day of the river,

Where I sat with a jackknife and quickly
Opened my sole to the water.
Blood shed for the sake of one's life

Takes on the hid shape of the channel,
Disappearing under logs and through boulders.
The freezing river poured on

And, as it took hold of my blood,
Leapt up round the rocks and boiled over.
I felt that my heart's blood could flow

Unendingly out of the mountain,
Splitting bedrock apart upon redness,
And the current of life at my instep

Give deathlessly as a spring.
Some leaves fell from trees and whirled under.
I saw my struck bloodstream assume,

Inside the cold path of the river,
The inmost routes of a serpent
Through grass, through branches and leaves.

When I rose, the live oaks were ashen
And the wild grass was dead without flame.
Through the blasted cornfield I hobbled,

My foot tied up in my shirt,
And met my old wife in the garden,
Where she reached for a withering apple.

I lay in the country and dreamed
Of the substance and course of the river
While the different colors of fever

Like quilt patches flickered upon me.
At last I arose, with the poison
Gone out of the seam of the scar,

And brought my wife eastward and weeping,
Through the copper fields springing alive
With the promise of harvest for no one.

Beginning to dangle beneath
The wind that blows from the undermined wood,
I feel the great pulley grind,

The thread I cling to lengthen
And let me soaring and spinning down into marble,
Hooked and weightlessly happy

Where the squared sun shines
Back equally from all four sides, out of stone
And years of dazzling labor,

To land at last among men
Who cut with power saws a Parian whiteness
And, chewing slow tobacco,

Their eyebrows like frost,
Shunt house-sized blocks and lash them to cables
And send them heavenward

Into small-town banks,
Into the columns and statues of government buildings,
But mostly graves.

I mount my monument and rise
Slowly and spinningly from the white-gloved men
Toward the hewn sky

Out of the basement of light,
Sadly, lifted through time's blinding layers
On perhaps my tombstone

In which the original shape
Michelangelo believed was in every rock upon earth
Is heavily stirring,

Surprised to be an angel,
To be waked in North Georgia by the ponderous play
Of men with ten-ton blocks

But no more surprised than I
To feel sadness fall off as though I myself
Were rising from stone

Held by a thread in midair,
Badly cut, local-looking, and totally uninspired,
Not a masterwork

Or even worth seeing at all
But the spirit of this place just the same,
Felt here as joy.

A FOLK SINGER OF THE THIRTIES

On a bed of gravel moving
Over the other gravel
Roadbed between the rails, I lay
As in my apartment now.
I felt the engine enter
A tunnel a half-mile away
And settled deeper
Into the stones of my sleep
Drifting through North Dakota.
I pulled them over me
For warmth, though it was summer,
And in the dark we pulled

Into the freight yards of Bismarck.
In the gravel car buried
To my nose in sledge-hammered stones,
My guitar beside me straining
Its breast beneath the rock,
I lay in the buzzing yards
And crimson hands swinging lights
Saw my closed eyes burn
Open and shine in their lanterns.
The yard bulls pulled me out,
Raining a rockslide of pebbles.
Bashed in the head, I lay

On the ground
As in my apartment now.
I spat out my teeth
Like corn, as they jerked me upright
To be an example for
The boys who would ride the freights
Looking for work, or for
Their American lives.
Four held me stretching against
The chalked red boards,
Spreading my hands and feet,
And nailed me to the boxcar

With twenty-penny nails.
I hung there open-mouthed
As though I had no more weight
Or voice. The train moved out.

Through the landscape I edged
And drifted, my head on my breast
As in my clean sheets now,
And went flying sideways through
The country, the rivers falling
Away beneath my safe
Immovable feet,
Close to me as they fell
Down under the boiling trestles,
And the fields and woods
Unfolded. Sometimes, behind me,
Going into the curves,
Cattle cried in unison,
Singing of stockyards
Where their tilted blood
Would be calmed and spilled.
I heard them until I sailed
Into the dark of the woods,
Flying always into the moonlight
And out again into rain
That filled my mouth
With a great life-giving word,
And into the many lights
The towns hung up for Christmas
Sales, the berries and tinsel,
And then out again
Into the countryside.
Everyone I passed

Could never believe what they saw,
But gave me one look
They would never forget, as I stood
In my overalls, stretched on the nails,
And went by, or stood
In the steaming night yards,

Waiting to couple on,
Overhanging the cattle coming
Into the cars from the night-lights.
The worst pain was when
We shuddered away from the platforms.
I lifted my head and croaked
Like a crow, and the nails
Vibrated with something like music
Endlessly clicking with movement
And the powerful, simple curves.
I learned where the oil lay
Under the fields,
Where the water ran
With the most industrial power,
Where the best corn would grow
And what manure to use
On any field that I saw.
If riches were there,
Whatever it was would light up
Like a bonfire seen through an eyelid
And begin to be words
That would go with the sound of the rails.
Ghostly bridges sprang up across rivers,
Mills towered where they would be,
Slums tottered, and buildings longed
To bear up their offices.
I hung for years
And in the end knew it all
Through pain: the land,
The future of profits and commerce
And also humility
Without which none of it mattered.
In the stockyards west of Chicago

One evening, the orphans assembled
Like choir boys
And drew the nails from my hands

And from my accustomed feet.
I stumbled with them to their homes
In Hooverville

And began to speak
In a chapel of galvanized tin
Of what one wishes for
When streaming alone into woods
And out into sunlight and moonlight
And when having a station lamp bulb
In one eye and not the other
And under the bites
Of snowflakes and clouds of flies
And the squandered dust of the prairies
That will not settle back
Beneath the crops.
In my head the farms
And industrial sites were burning
To produce.
One night, I addressed the A.A.,
Almost singing,
And in the fiery,
Unconsummated desire
For drink that rose around me
From those mild-mannered men,
I mentioned a place for a shoe store
That I had seen near the yards
As a blackened hulk with potential.
A man rose up,
Took a drink from a secret bottle,
And hurried out of the room.
A year later to the day
He knelt at my feet
In a silver suit of raw silk.
I sang to industrial groups
With a pearl-inlaid guitar

And plucked the breast-straining strings
With a nail that had stood through my hand.

I could not keep silent
About the powers of water,
Or where the coal beds lay quaking,
Or where electrical force
Should stalk in its roofless halls
Alone through the night wood,
Where the bridges should leap,
Striving with all their might
To connect with the other shore
To carry the salesmen.
I gave all I knew
To the owners, and they went to work.
I waked, not buried in pebbles

Behind the tank car,
But in the glimmering steeple
That sprang as I said it would
And lifted the young married couples,
Clutching their credit cards,
Boldly into and out of
Their American lives.
I said to myself that the poor
Would always be poor until
The towers I knew of should rise
And the oil be tapped:
That I had literally sung
My sick country up from its deathbed,
But nothing would do,
No logical right holds the truth.
In the sealed rooms I think of this,
Recording the nursery songs
In a checkered and tailored shirt,
As a guest on TV shows
And in my apartment now:
This is all a thing I began
To believe, to change, and to sell
When I opened my mouth to the rich.

III

THE BEING

I
It is there, above him, beyond, behind,

Distant, and near where he lies in his sleep
Bound down as for warranted torture.
Through his eyelids he sees it

Drop off its wings or its clothes.
He groans, and breaks almost from

Or into another sleep.
Something fills the bed he has been
Able only to half-fill.

He turns and buries his head.

II
Moving down his back,
Back up his back,
Is an infinite, unworldly frankness,
Showing him what an entire

Possession nakedness is.
Something over him

Is praying.
     It reaches down under
His eyelids and gently lifts them.
He expects to look straight into eyes
And to see thereby through the roof.

III
Darkness. The windowpane stirs.
His lids close again, and the room

Begins to breathe on him
As through the eyeholes of a mask.

The praying of prayer
Is not in the words but the breath.

It sees him and touches him
All over, from everywhere.
It lifts him from the mattress
To be able to flow around him

In the heat from a coal bed burning
Far under the earth.
He enters—enters with . . .

What? His tongue? A word?
His own breath? Some part of his body?
All.
                              None.

He lies laughing silently
In the dark of utter delight.

        IV
It glides, glides
Lightly over him, over his chest and legs.
All breath is called suddenly back

Out of laughter and weeping at once.
His face liquefies and freezes

Like a mask. He goes rigid
And breaks into sweat from his heart
All over his body

In something's hands.

        V
He sleeps, and the windowpane
Ceases to flutter.

Frost crawls down off it
And backs into only
The bottom two corners of glass.

VI

He stirs, with the sun held at him
Out of late-winter dawn, and blazing
Levelly into his face.
He blazes back with his eyes closed,
Given, also, renewed

Fertility, to raise
Dead plants and half-dead beasts

Out of their thawing holes,
And children up,
From mortal women or angels,
As true to themselves as he

Is only in visited darkness
For one night out of the year,

And as he is now, seeing straight
Through the roof   wide   wider

Wide awake.

All things that go deep enough
Into rain and cold
Take on, before they break down,
A shining in every part.
The necks of slender trees
Reel under it, too much crowned,
Like princes dressing as kings,

And the redwoods let sink their branches
Like arms that try to hold buckets
Filling slowly with diamonds

Until a cannon goes off
Somewhere inside the still trunk
And a limb breaks, just before midnight,
Plunging houses into the darkness
And hands into cupboards, all seeking
Candles, and finding each other.
There is this skin

Always waiting in cold-enough air.
I have seen aircraft, in war,
Squatting on runways,

Dazed with their own enclosed,
Coming-forth, intensified color
As though seen by a child in a poem.
I have felt growing over
Me in the heated death rooms
Of uncles, the ice
Skin, that which the dying

Lose, and we others,
In their thawing presence, take on.
I have felt the heroic glaze

Also, in hospital waiting
Rooms: that masterly shining

And the slow weight that makes you sit
Like an emperor, fallen, becoming
His monument, with the stiff thorns
Of fear upside down on the brow,
An overturned kingdom:

Through the window of ice
I have stared at my son in his cage,
Just born, just born.

I touched the frost of my eyebrows
To the cold he turned to
Blindly, but sensing a thing.
Neither glass nor the jagged
Helm on my forehead would melt.
My son now stands with his head
At my shoulder. I

Stand, stooping more, but the same,
Not knowing whether
I will break before I can feel,

Before I can give up my powers,
Or whether the ice light
In my eyes will ever snap off
Before I die. I am still,
And my son, doing what he was taught,
Listening hard for a buried cannon,
Stands also, calm as glass.

Bums, on waking,
Do not always find themselves
In gutters with water running over their legs
And the pillow of the curbstone
Turning hard as sleep drains from it.
Mostly, they do not know

But hope for where they shall come to.
The opening of the eye is precious,

And the shape of the body also,
Lying as it has fallen,
Disdainfully crumpling earthward
Out of alcohol.
Drunken under their eyelids
Like children sleeping toward Christmas,

They wait for the light to shine
Wherever it may decide.

Often it brings them staring
Through glass in the rich part of town,
Where the forms of humanized wax
Are arrested in midstride
With their heads turned, and dressed
By force. This is ordinary, and has come

To be disappointing.
They expect and hope for

Something totally other:
That while they staggered last night
For hours, they got clear,
Somehow, of the city; that they
Have burst through a hedge, and are lying
In a trampled rose garden,

Pillowed on a bulldog's side,
A watchdog's, whose breathing

Is like the earth's, unforced—
Or that they may, once a year
(Any dawn now), awaken
In church, not on the coffin boards
Of a back pew, or on furnace-room rags,
But on the steps of the altar

Where candles are opening their eyes
With all-seeing light

And the green stained glass of the windows
Falls on them like sanctified leaves.
Who else has quite the same
Commitment to not being sure
What he shall behold, come from sleep—
A child, a policeman, an effigy?

Who else has died and thus risen?
Never knowing how they have got there,

They might just as well have walked
On water, through walls, out of graves,
Through potter's fields and through barns,
Through slums where their stony pillows
Refused to harden, because of
Their hope for this morning's first light,

With water moving over their legs
More like living cover than it is.

Through rain falling on us no faster
Than it runs down the wall we go through,
My son and I shed Paris like a skin
And slip into a cage to say goodbye.
Through a hole in the wall
Of the Jardin des Plantes
We come to go round

The animals for the last time;
Tomorrow we set out for home.
For some reason it is the snakes
To which we seem to owe
The longest farewell of our lives.
These have no bars, but drift
On an island held still by a moat,

Unobstructedly gazing out.
My son will not move from watching
Them through the dust of cold water,
And neither will I, when I realize
That this is my farewell
To Europe also. I begin to look
More intently than I ever have.

In the moat one is easily swimming
Like the essence of swimming itself,
Pure line and confident curve
Requiring no arms or legs.
In a tree, a bush, there is one
Whose body is living there motionless,
Emotionless, with drops running down,

His slack tail holding a small
Growing gem that will not fall.
I can see one's eyes in the brush,
As fixed as a portrait's,

Gazing into, discovering, forgetting
The heart of all rainfall and sorrow.
He licks at the air,

Tasting the carded water
Changed by the leaves of his home.
The rain stops in midair before him
Mesmerized as a bird—
A harmony of drops in which I see
Towers and churches, domes,
Capitals, streets like the shining

Paths of the Jardin des Plantes,
All old, all cold with my gaze
In glittering, unearthly fascination.
I say, "Yes! So I have seen them!
But I have brought also the human,
The presence of self and of love."
Yet it is not so. My son shifts

Uneasily back and away, bored now,
A tourist to the bitter end,
And I know I have not been moved
Enough by the things I have moved through,
And I have seen what I have seen

Unchanged, hypnotized, and perceptive:
The jewelled branches,
The chandeliers, the windows
Made for looking through only when weeping,
The continent hazy with grief,
The water in the air without support
Sustained in the serpent's eye.

A moment tries to come in
Through the windows, when one must go
Beyond what there is in the room,

But it must come straight down.
Lord, it is time,

And I must get up and start
To circle through my father's empty house
Looking for things to put on
Or to strip myself of
So that I can fall to my knees
And produce a word I can't say
Until all my reason is slain.

Here is the gray sweater
My father wore in the cold,
The snapped threads growing all over it
Like his gray body hair.
The spurs of his gamecocks glimmer
Also, in my light, dry hand.
And here is the head of a boar
I once helped to kill with two arrows:

Two things of my father's
Wild, Bible-reading life
And my own best and stillest moment
In a hog's head waiting for glory.

All these I set up in the attic,
The boar's head, gaffs, and the sweater
On a chair, and gaze in the dark
Up into the boar's painted gullet.

Nothing. Perhaps I should feel more foolish,
Even, than this.
I put on the ravelled nerves

And gray hairs of my tall father
In the dry grave growing like fleece,
Strap his bird spurs to my heels
And kneel down under the skylight.
I put on the hollow hog's head
Gazing straight up
With star points in the glass eyes
That would blind anything that looked in

And cause it to utter words.
The night sky fills with a light

Of hunting: with leaves
And sweat and the panting of dogs

Where one tries hard to draw breath,
A single breath, and hold it.
I draw the breath of life
For the dead hog:
I catch it from the still air,
Hold it in the boar's rigid mouth,
And see

>A young aging man with a bow
>And a green arrow pulled to his cheek
>Standing deep in a mountain creek bed,
>Stiller than trees or stones,
>Waiting and staring

Beasts, angels
I am nearly that motionless now

>There is a frantic leaping at my sides
>Of dogs coming out of the water

The moon and the stars do not move

>I bare my teeth, and my mouth
>Opens, a foot long, popping with tushes

A word goes through my closed lips

> *I gore a dog, he falls, falls back*
> *Still snapping, turns away and dies*
> *While swimming. I feel each hair on my back*
> *Stand up through the eye of a needle*

Where the hair was
On my head stands up
As if it were there

> *The man is still; he is stiller: still*

Yes.

> *Something comes out of him*
> *Like a shaft of sunlight or starlight.*
> *I go forward toward him*

(Beasts, angels)

> *With light standing through me,*
> *Covered with dogs, but the water*
> *Tilts to the sound of the bowstring*

The planets attune all their orbits

> *The sound from his fingers,*
> *Like a plucked word, quickly pierces*
> *Me again, the trees try to dance*
> *Clumsily out of the wood*

I have said something else

> *And underneath, underwater,*
> *In the creek bed are dancing*
> *The sleepy pebbles*

The universe is creaking like boards
Thumping with heartbeats
And bonebeats

And every image of death
In my head turns red with blood.
The man of blood does not move

My father is pale on my body

The dogs of blood
Hang to my ears,
The shadowy bones of the limbs
The sun lays on the water
Mass darkly together

Moonlight, moonlight

The sun mounts my hackles
And I fall; I roll
In the water;
My tongue spills blood
Bound for the ocean;
It moves away, and I see
The trees strain and part, see him
Look upward

Inside the hair helmet
I look upward out of the total
Stillness of killing with arrows.
I have seen the hog see me kill him
And I was as still as I hoped.
I am that still now, and now.
My father's sweater
Swarms over me in the dark.
I see nothing, but for a second

Something goes through me
Like an accident, a negligent glance,

Like the explosion of a star
Six billion light years off
Whose light gives out

Just as it goes straight through me.
The boar's blood is sailing through rivers
Bearing the living image
Of my most murderous stillness.
It picks up speed
And my heart pounds.
The chicken-blood rust at my heels
Freshens, as though near a death wound
Or flight. I nearly lift
From the floor, from my father's grave
Crawling over my chest,

And then get up
In the way I usually do.
I take off the head of the hog
And the gaffs and the panting sweater
And go down the dusty stairs
And never come back.

I don't know quite what has happened
Or that anything has,

Hoping only that
The irrelevancies one thinks of
When trying to pray
Are the prayer,

And that I have got by my own
Means to the hovering place
Where I can say with any
Other than the desert fathers—
Those who saw angels come,
Their body glow shining on bushes
And sheep's wool and animal eyes,
To answer what questions men asked

In Heaven's tongue,
Using images of earth
Almightily:

PROPHECIES, FIRE IN THE SINFUL TOWERS,
WASTE AND FRUITION IN THE LAND,
CORN, LOCUSTS AND ASHES,
THE LION'S SKULL PULSING WITH HONEY,
THE BLOOD OF THE FIRST-BORN,
A GIRL MADE PREGNANT WITH A GLANCE
LIKE AN EXPLODING STAR
AND A CHILD BORN OF UTTER LIGHT—

Where I can say only, and truly,
That my stillness was violent enough,
That my brain had blood enough,
That my right hand was steady enough,
That the warmth of my father's wool grave
Imparted love enough
And the keen heels of feathery slaughter
Provided lift enough,
That reason was dead enough
For something important to be:

That, if not heard,
It may have been somehow said.

IV

THE DRIVER

At the end of the war I arose
From my bed in the tent and walked
Where the island fell through white stones
Until it became the green sea.
Into light that dazzled my brain
Like the new thought of peace, I walked
Until I was swimming and singing.

Over the foundered landing craft
That took the island, I floated,
And then like a thistle came
On the deep wind of water to rest
Far out, my long legs of shadow down-
pointing to ground where my soul
Could take root and spring as it must.

Below me a rusted halftrack
Moved in the depths with the movement
One sees a thing take through tears
Of joy, or terrible sorrow,
A thing which in quietness lies
Beyond both. Slowly I sank
And slid into the driver's shattered seat.

Driving through the country of the drowned
On a sealed secret-keeping breath,
Ten feet under water, I sat still,
Getting used to the burning stare
Of the wide-eyed dead after battle.
I saw, through the sensitive roof—
The uneasy, lyrical skin that lies

Between death and life, trembling always—
An airplane come over, perfectly

Soundless, but could not tell
Why I lived, or why I was sitting,
With my lungs being shaped like two bells,
At the wheel of a craft in a wave
Of attack that broke upon coral.

"I become pure spirit," I tried
To say, in a bright smoke of bubbles,
But I was becoming no more
Than haunted, for to be so
Is to sink out of sight, and to lose
The power of speech in the presence
Of the dead, with the eyes turning green,

And to leap at last for the sky
Very nearly too late, where another
Leapt and could not break into
His breath, where it lay, in battle
As in peace, available, secret,
Dazzling and huge, filled with sunlight,
For thousands of miles on the water.

In the war where many men fell
Wind blew in a ring, and was grass.
Many horses fell also to rifles
On a track in the Philippine Islands
And divided their still, wiry meat
To be eaten by prisoners.
I sat at the finish line
At the end of the war

Knowing that I would live.
Long grass went around me, half wind,
Where I rode the rail of the infield
And the dead horses travelled in waves
On past the finishing post.
Dead wind lay down in live grass,
The flowers, pounding like hooves,
Stood up in the sun and were still,

And my mind, like a fence on fire,
Went around those unknown men:
Those who tore from the red, light bones
The intensified meat of hunger
And then lay down open-eyed
In a raw, straining dream of new life.
Joy entered the truth and flowed over
As the wind rose out of the grass

Leaping with red and white flowers:
Joy in the bone-strewn infield
Where clouds of barbed wire contained
Men who ran in a vision of greenness,
Sustained by the death of beasts,
On the tips of the sensitive grass blades,
Each footstep putting forth petals,
Their bones light and strong as the wind.

From the fence I dropped off and waded
Knee-deep in the billowing homestretch
And picked up the red of one flower.
It beat in my hand like my heart,
Filled with the pulse of the air,
And I felt my long thighbones yearn
To leap with the trained, racing dead.
When beasts are fallen in wars

For food, men seeking a reason to live
Stand mired in the on-going grass
And sway there, sweating and thinking,
With fire coming out of their brains
Like the thought of food and life
Of prisoners. When death moves close
In the night, I think I can kill it:
Let a man let his mind burn and change him

To one who was prisoner here
As he sings in his sleep in his home,
His mane streaming over the pillows,
The white threads of time
Mixed with the hair of his temples,
His grave-grass risen without him:
Now, in the green of that sleep,
Let him start the air of the island

From the tangled gate of jute string
That hangs from the battered grandstand
Where hope comes from animal blood
And the hooves of ghosts become flowers
That a captive may run as in Heaven:
Let him strip the dead shirt from his chest
And, sighing like all saved men,
Take his nude child in his arms.

DRINKING FROM A HELMET

I

I climbed out, tired of waiting
For my foxhole to turn in the earth
On its side or its back for a grave,
And got in line
Somewhere in the roaring of dust.
Every tree on the island was nowhere,
Blasted away.

II

In the middle of combat, a graveyard
Was advancing after the troops
With laths and balls of string;
Grass already tinged it with order.
Between the new graves and the foxholes
A green water-truck stalled out.
I moved up on it, behind
The hill that cut off the firing.

III

My turn, and I shoved forward
A helmet I picked from the ground,
Not daring to take mine off
Where somebody else may have come
Loose from the steel of his head.

IV

Keeping the foxhole doubled
In my body and begging
For water, safety, and air,
I drew water out of the truckside
As if dreaming the helmet full.
In my hands, the sun
Came on in a feathery light.

V

In midair, water trimming
To my skinny dog-faced look

Showed my life's first all-out beard
Growing wildly, escaping from childhood,
Like the beards of the dead, all now
Underfoot beginning to grow.
Selected ripples wove through it,
Knocked loose with a touch from all sides
Of a brain killed early that morning,
Most likely, and now
In its absence holding
My sealed, sunny image from harm,
Weighing down my hands,
Shipping at the edges,
Too heavy on one side, then the other.

VI

I drank, with the timing of rust.
A vast military wedding
Somewhere advanced one step.

VII

All around, equipment drifting in light,
Men drinking like cattle and bushes,
Cans, leather, canvas and rifles,
Grass pouring down from the sun
And up from the ground.
Grass: and the summer advances
Invisibly into the tropics.
Wind, and the summer shivers
Through many men standing or lying
In the GI gardener's hand
Spreading and turning green
All over the hill.

VIII

At the middle of water
Bright circles dawned inward and outward
Like oak rings surviving the tree
As its soul, or like

The concentric gold spirit of time.
I kept trembling forward through something
Just born of me.

IX

My nearly dead power to pray
Like an army increased and assembled,
As when, in a harvest of sparks,
The helmet leapt from the furnace
And clamped itself
On the heads of a billion men.
Some words directed to Heaven
Went through all the strings of the graveyard
Like a message that someone sneaked in,
Tapping a telegraph key
At dead of night, then running
For his life.

X

I swayed, as if kissed in the brain.
Above the shelled palm-stumps I saw
How the tops of huge trees might be moved
In a place in my own country
I never had seen in my life.
In the closed dazzle of my mouth
I fought with a word in the water
To call on the dead to strain
Their muscles to get up and go there.
I felt the difference between
Sweat and tears when they rise,
Both trying to melt the brow down.

XI

On even the first day of death
The dead cannot rise up,
But their last thought hovers somewhere
For whoever finds it.
My uninjured face floated strangely
In the rings of a bodiless tree.
Among them, also, a final

Idea lived, waiting
As in Ariel's limbed, growing jail.

XII

I stood as though I possessed
A cool, trembling man
Exactly my size, swallowed whole.
Leather swung at his waist,
Web-cord, buckles, and metal,
Crouching over the dead
Where they waited for all their hands
To be connected like grass-roots.

XIII

In the brown half-life of my beard
The hair stood up
Like the awed hair lifting the back
Of a dog that has eaten a swan.
Now light like this
Staring into my face
Was the first thing around me at birth.
Be no more killed, it said.

XIV

The wind in the grass
Moved gently in secret flocks,
Then spread to be
Nothing, just where they were.
In delight's
Whole shining condition and risk,
I could see how my body might come
To be imagined by something
That thought of it only for joy.

XV

Fresh sweat and unbearable tears
Drawn up by my feet from the field
Between my eyebrows became
One thing at last,
And I could cry without hiding.

The world dissolved into gold;
I could have stepped up into air.
I drank and finished
Like tasting of Heaven,
Which is simply of,
At seventeen years,
Not dying wherever you are.

XVI

Enough
Shining, I picked up my carbine and said.
I threw my old helmet down
And put the wet one on.
Warmed water ran over my face.
My last thought changed, and I knew
I inherited one of the dead.

XVII

I saw tremendous trees
That would grow on the sun if they could,
Towering. I saw a fence
And two boys facing each other,
Quietly talking,
Looking in at the gigantic redwoods,
The rings in the trunks turning slowly
To raise up stupendous green.
They went away, one turning
The wheels of a blue bicycle,
The smaller one curled catercornered
In the handlebar basket.

XVIII

I would survive and go there,
Stepping off the train in a helmet
That held a man's last thought,
Which showed him his older brother
Showing him trees.
I would ride through all
California upon two wheels
Until I came to the white

Dirt road where they had been,
Hoping to meet his blond brother,
And to walk with him into the wood
Until we were lost,
Then take off the helmet
And tell him where I had stood,
What poured, what spilled, what swallowed:

XIX
And tell him I was the man.

Buckdancer's Choice

To Maibelle Swift Dickey and Eugene Dickey
life-givers

THE FIREBOMBING

Denke daran, dass nach den grossen
    Zerstörungen
Jedermann beweisen wird, dass er
    unshuldig war.
           —*Günter Eich*
Or hast thou an arm like God?
           —*The Book of Job*

Homeowners unite.

All families lie together, though some are burned alive.
The others try to feel
For them. Some can, it is often said.

Starve and take off

Twenty years in the suburbs, and the palm trees willingly leap
Into the flashlights,
And there is beneath them also
A booted crackling of snailshells and coral sticks.
There are cowl flaps and the tilt cross of propellers,
The shovel-marked clouds' far sides against the moon,
The enemy filling up the hills
With ceremonial graves. At my somewhere among these,

Snap, a bulb is tricked on in the cockpit

And some technical-minded stranger with my hands
Is sitting in a glass treasure-hole of blue light,
Having potential fire under the undeodorized arms
Of his wings, on thin bomb-shackles,
The "tear-drop-shaped" 300-gallon drop-tanks
Filled with napalm and gasoline.

Thinking forward ten minutes
From that, there is also the burst straight out

Of the overcast into the moon; there is now
The moon-metal-shine of propellers, the quarter-
moonstone, aimed at the waves,
Stopped on the cumulus.

There is then this re-entry
Into cloud, for the engines to ponder their sound.
In white dark the aircraft shrinks; Japan

Dilates around it like a thought.
Coming out, the one who is here is over
Land, passing over the all-night grainfields,
In dark paint over
The woods with one silver side,
Rice-water calm at all levels
Of the terraced hill.
                          Enemy rivers and trees
Sliding off me like snakeskin,
Strips of vapor spooled from the wingtips
Going   invisible   passing   over   on
Over   bridges   roads for nightwalkers
Sunday night in the enemy's country   absolute
Calm   the moon's face   coming   slowly
About
          the inland sea
Slants   is woven with wire thread
Levels out   holds together like a quilt
Off the starboard wing   cloud flickers
At my glassed-off forehead   the moon's now and again
Uninterrupted face going forward
Over the waves in a glide-path
Lost into land.

Going: going with it

Combat booze by my side in a cratered canteen,
Bourbon frighteningly mixed
With GI pineapple juice,
Dogs trembling under me for hundreds of miles, on many
Islands, sleep-smelling that ungodly mixture

Of napalm and high-octane fuel,
Good bourbon and GI juice.

Rivers circling behind me around
Come to the fore, and bring
A town with everyone darkened.
Five thousand people are sleeping off
An all-day American drone.
Twenty years in the suburbs have not shown me
Which ones were hit and which not.

Haul on the wheel   racking slowly
The aircraft blackly around
In a dark dream   that   that is
That is like flying inside someone's head

Think of this   think of this

I did not think of my house
But think of my house now

Where the lawn mower rests on its laurels
Where the diet exists
For my own good   where I try to drop
Twenty years, eating figs in the pantry
Blinded by each and all
Of the eye-catching cans that gladly have caught my wife's eye
Until I cannot say
Where the screwdriver is   where the children
Get off the bus   where the new
Scoutmaster lives   where the fly
Hones his front legs   where the hammock folds
Its erotic daydreams   where the Sunday
School text for the day has been put   where the fire
Wood is   where the payments
For everything under the sun
Pile peacefully up,

But in this half-paid-for pantry
Among the red lids that screw off

With an easy half-twist to the left
And the long drawers crammed with dim spoons,
I still have charge—secret charge—
Of the fire developed to cling
To everything: to golf carts and fingernail
Scissors as yet unborn   tennis shoes
Grocery baskets   toy fire engines
New Buicks stalled by the half-moon
Shining at midnight on crossroads   green paint
Of jolly garden tools   red Christmas ribbons:

Not atoms, these, but glue inspired
By love of country to burn,
The apotheosis of gelatin.

Behind me having risen the Southern Cross
Set up by chaplains in the Ryukyus—
Orion, Scorpio, the immortal silver
Like the myths of king-
insects at swarming time—
One mosquito, dead drunk
On altitude, drones on, far under the engines,
And bites between
The oxygen mask and the eye.
The enemy-colored skin of families
Determines to hold its color
In sleep, as my hand turns whiter
Than ever, clutching the toggle—
The ship shakes   bucks
Fire hangs   not yet fire
In the air above Beppu
For I am fulfilling

An "anti-morale" raid upon it.
All leashes of dogs
Break under the first bomb, around those
In bed, or late in the public baths: around those
Who inch forward on their hands
Into medicinal waters.
Their heads come up with a roar

184

Of Chicago fire:
Come up with the carp pond showing
The bathhouse upside down,
Standing stiller to show it more
As I sail artistically over
The resort town followed by farms,
Singing and twisting
All the handles in heaven   kicking
The small cattle off their feet
In a red costly blast
Flinging jelly over the walls
As in a chemical war-
fare field demonstration.
With fire of mine like a cat

Holding onto another man's walls,
My hat should crawl on my head
In streetcars, thinking of it,
The fat on my body should pale.

Gun down
The engines, the eight blades sighing
For the moment when the roofs will connect
Their flames, and make a town burning with all
American fire.
                    Reflections of houses catch;
Fire shuttles from pond to pond
In every direction, till hundreds flash with one death.
With this in the dark of the mind,
Death will not be what it should;
Will not, even now, even when
My exhaled face in the mirror
Of bars, dilates in a cloud like Japan.
The death of children is ponds
Shutter-flashing; responding mirrors; it climbs
The terraces of hills
Smaller and smaller, a mote of red dust
At a hundred feet; at a hundred and one it goes out.
That is what should have got in
To my eye

And shown the insides of houses, the low tables
Catch fire from the floor mats,
Blaze up in gas around their heads
Like a dream of suddenly growing
Too intense for war. Ah, under one's dark arms
Something strange-scented falls—when those on earth
Die, there is not even sound;
One is cool and enthralled in the cockpit,
Turned blue by the power of beauty,
In a pale treasure-hole of soft light
Deep in aesthetic contemplation,
Seeing the ponds catch fire
And cast it through ring after ring
Of land: O death in the middle
Of acres of inch-deep water!   Useless

Firing   small arms
Speckles   from the river
Bank   one ninety-millimeter
Misses   far down   wrong petals   gone

It is this detachment,
The honored aesthetic evil,
The greatest sense of power in one's life,
That must be shed in bars, or by whatever
Means, by starvation
Visions in well-stocked pantries:
The moment when the moon sails in between
The tail-booms   the rudders nod   I swing
Over   directly over the heart
The *heart* of the fire. A mosquito burns out on my cheek
With the cold of my face   there are the eyes
In blue light   bar light
All masked but them   the moon
Crossing from left to right   in the streams below
Oriental fish form quickly
In the chemical shine,
In their eyes one tiny seed
Of deranged, Old Testament light.

Letting go   letting go
The plane rises gently   dark forms
Glide off me   long water   pales
In safe zones   a new cry enters
The voice box of chained family dogs

We buck   leap over something
Not there   settle back
Leave it   leave it clinging and crying
It consumes them in a hot
Body-flash, old age or menopause
Of children, clings and burns
                              eating through
And when a reed mat catches fire
From me, it explodes through field after field
Bearing its sleeper   another

Bomb finds a home
And clings to it like a child. And so

Goodbye to the grassy mountains
To cloud streaming from the night engines
Flags   pennons   curved silks
Of air   myself streaming also
My body covered
With flags, the air of flags
Between the engines.
Forever I do sleep in that position,
Forever in a turn
For home that breaks out streaming banners
From my wingtips,
Wholly in position to admire.

O then I knock it off
And turn for home over the black complex thread worked through
The silver night-sea,
Following the huge, moon-washed steppingstones
Of the Ryukyus south,
The nightgrass of mountains billowing softly

In my rising heat.
                    Turn and tread down
The yellow stones of the islands
To where Okinawa burns,
Pure gold, on the radar screen,
Beholding, beneath, the actual island form
In the vast water-silver poured just above solid ground,
An inch of water extending for thousands of miles
Above flat ploughland. Say "down," and it is done.

All this, and I am still hungry,
Still twenty years overweight, still unable
To get down there or see
What really happened.
                      But it may be that I could not,
If I tried, say to any
Who lived there, deep in my flames: say, in cold
Grinning sweat, as to another
As these homeowners who are always curving
Near me down the different-grassed street: say
As though to the neighbor
I borrowed the hedge-clippers from
On the darker-grassed side of the two,
Come in, my house is yours, come in
If you can, if you
Can pass this unfired door. It is that I can imagine
At the threshold nothing
With its ears crackling off
Like powdery leaves,
Nothing with children of ashes, nothing not
Amiable, gentle, well-meaning,
A little nervous for no
Reason   a little worried   a little too loud
Or too easygoing   nothing I haven't lived with
For twenty years, still nothing not as
American as I am, and proud of it.

Absolution? Sentence? No matter;
The thing itself is in that.

II

BUCKDANCER'S CHOICE

So I would hear out those lungs,
The air split into nine levels,
Some gift of tongues of the whistler

In the invalid's bed: my mother,
Warbling all day to herself
The thousand variations of one song;

It is called Buckdancer's Choice.
For years, they have all been dying
Out, the classic buck-and-wing men

Of traveling minstrel shows;
With them also an old woman
Was dying of breathless angina,

Yet still found breath enough
To whistle up in my head
A sight like a one-man band,

Freed black, with cymbals at heel,
An ex-slave who thrivingly danced
To the ring of his own clashing light

Through the thousand variations of one song
All day to my mother's prone music,
The invalid's warbler's note,

While I crept close to the wall
Sock-footed, to hear the sounds alter,
Her tongue like a mockingbird's break

Through stratum after stratum of a tone
Proclaiming what choices there are
For the last dancers of their kind,

For ill women and for all slaves
Of death, and children enchanted at walls
With a brass-beating glow underfoot,

Not dancing but nearly risen
Through barnlike, theatrelike houses
On the wings of the buck and wing.

Faces seen once are seen

To fade from around one feature,
Leaving a chin, a scar, an expression

Forever in the air beneath a streetlight,
Glancing in boredom from the window
Of a bus in a country town,
Showing teeth for a moment only,
All of which die out of mind, except
One silver one.

Who had the dog-bitten ear?
The granulated lids? The birthmark?

Faces seen once change always

Into and out of each other:
An eye you saw in Toulon
Is gazing at you down a tin drainpipe
You played with as a dull child
In Robertstown, Georgia.
There it is April; the one eye

Concentrates, the rusty pipe

Is trembling; behind the eye
Is a pine tree blurring with tears:

You and someone's blue eye
Transforming your boyhood are weeping
For an only son drowned in warm water
With the French fleet off Senegal.
Soon after, the cancer-clamped face
Of your great-grandfather relaxes,

Smiles again with the lips of a newsboy.
Faces seen once make up

One face being organized

And changed and known less all the time,
Unsexed, amorphous, growing in necessity
As you deepen in age.
The brow wrinkles, a blind, all-knowing
Questioning look comes over it,
And every face in the street begins

To partake of the look in the eyes,

Every nose is part of that nose
And changes the nose; every innocence and every

Unspoken-of guilt goes into it,
Into the face of the one
Encountered, unknowable person who waits
For you all over the world
In coffee shops, filling stations, bars,
In mills and orphan asylums,

In hospitals, prisons, at parties,
Yearning to be one thing.

At your death, they—it is there,

And the features congeal,
Having taken the last visage in,
Over you, pretesting its smile,
The skin the indwelling no
Color of all colors mingled,
The eyes asking all there is.

Composed, your own face trembles near

Joining that other, knowing
That finally something must break

Or speak. A silver tooth gleams;
You mumble, whispering "You

Are human, are what I have witnessed.
You are all faces seen once."
Through the bent, staring, unstable dark
Of a drainpipe, Unity hears you—

A God-roar of hearing—say only
"You are an angel's too-realized

Unbearable memoryless face."

THE COMMON GRAVE

I

Some sit and stare
In an unknown direction, though most lie still,
Knowing that every season
Must be wintered.

II

The mover of mists and streams
Is usually in the weeds
By twilight, taking slowly
A dark dedicated field-shape.

III

Of all those who are under,
Many are looking over
Their shoulder, although it is only one leap
To beyond-reason gold, only one
Breath to the sun's great city.
All ages of mankind unite
Where it is dark enough.

IV

The midstrides of out-of-shape runners,
The discarded strokes of bad swimmers,
Open-mouthed at the wrong time—
All these are hooked wrongly together.
A rumor runs through them like roots:
They must try even harder
To bring into their vast,
Indiscriminate embrace
All of humanity.

V

In someone's hand an acorn
Pulses, thinking
It is only one leap,
Only one.

VI

In the field by twilight are
The faller in leaves through October,
The white-headed flyer in thistles
Finding out secret currents of air,
The raiser of mists from the creekbed,
A fish extending his body
Through all the curves of the river,
The incredible moon in the voice box
Of dogs on All Souls' Night.

VII

All creatures tumbled together
Get back in their wildest arms
No single thing but each other,
Hear only sounds like train sounds,
Cattle sounds, earth-shakers.

VIII

The mover of all things struggles
In the green-crowded, green-crowned nightmare
Of a great king packed in an acorn.
A train bends round a curve
Like a fish. An oak tree breaks
Out and shoves for the moonlight,
Bearing leaves which shall murmur for years,
Dumfoundedly, like mouths opened all at once
At just the wrong time to be heard,
    Others, others.

REINCARNATION (I)

Still, passed through the spokes of an old wheel, on and around
The hub's furry rust in the weeds and shadows of the riverbank,
This one is feeling his life as a man move slowly away.
Fallen from that estate, he has gone down on his knees
And beyond, disappearing into the egg buried under the sand

And wakened to the low world being born, consisting now
Of the wheel on its side not turning, but leaning to rot away
In the sun a few feet farther off than it is for any man.
The roots bulge quietly under the earth beneath him;
With his tongue he can hear them in their concerted effort

To raise something, anything, out of the dark of the ground.
He has come by gliding, by inserting the head between stems.
Everything follows that as naturally as the creation
Of the world, leaving behind arms and legs, leaving behind
The intervals between tracks, leaving one long wavering step

In sand and none in grass: he moves through, moving nothing,
And the grass stands as never entered. It is in the new
Life of resurrection that one can come in one's own time
To a place like a rotting wheel, the white paint flaking from it,
Rust slowly emerging, and coil halfway through it, stopped

By a just administration of light and dark over the diamonds
Of the body. Here, also naturally growing, is a flat leaf
To rest the new head upon. The stem bends but knows the weight
And does not touch the ground, holding the snub, patterned face
Swaying with the roots of things. Inside the jaws, saliva

Has turned ice cold, drawn from bird eggs and thunderstruck rodents,
Dusty pine needles, blunt stones, horse dung, leaf mold,
But mainly, now, from waiting—all the time a symbol of evil—
Not for food, but for the first man to walk by the gentle river:
Minute by minute the head becomes more poisonous and poised.

Here in the wheel is the place to wait, with the eyes unclosable,
Unanswerable, the tongue occasionally listening, this time
No place in the body desiring to burn the tail away or to warn,
But only to pass on, handless, what yet may be transferred
In a sudden giving-withdrawing move, like a county judge striking a
    match.

THEM, CRYING

In the well-fed cage-sound of diesels,
Here, in the cab's boxed wind,
He is called to by something beyond
His life. In the sun's long haul
Of light, each week at this place,
He sings to the truck's eight wheels

But at night it is worse than useless:
The great building shoots and holds

Its rays, and he hears, through the engine,
Through the killed words of his own song,
Them: them crying. Unmarried, unchildlike,
Half-bearded and foul-mouthed, he feels
His hands lean away to the right
And bear the truck spiraling down

To the four streets going around
And around and around the hospital.

He sits, and the voices are louder,
An awakening, part-song sound
Calling anyone out of the life
He thought he led: a sound less than twelve
Years old, which wakes to the less-than-nothing
Of a bent glass straw in a glass

With small sleepless bubbles stuck to it:
Which feels a new mouth sewn shut

In a small body's back or its side
And would free some angelic voice
From the black crimped thread,
The snipped cat-whiskers of a wound—
A sound that can find no way
To beat the huge, orderly flowers.

At one-thirty he is drawn in,
Drawn in, drawn in and in,

Listening, through dozens of Bakelite floors
And walls, brogan-stepping along
Through green-tiled nightlighted rooms
Where implements bake in glass cases,
Through halls full of cloudy test tubes,
Up and down self-service elevators

That open both sides at once,
Through closets of lubricants,

Through a black beehive of typed labels,
Through intimate theatres
Scrubbed down with Lysol and salt,
Through a sordid district of pails,
Until, on the third floor rear
Of the donated Southeast Wing,

He comes on a man holding wrongly
A doll with feigning-closed eyes,

And a fat woman, hat in her lap,
Has crashed through a chairback to sleep.
Unbelonging, he circles their circle;
Then, as though a stitch broke
In his stomach, he wheels and goes through
The double-frosted warning-marked door.

Twelve parents at bay intone
In the brain waves that wash around heroes:

> Come, stripped to your T-shirt sleeves,
> Your coveralls, blue jeans, or chains,
> Your helmets or thickening haircuts,

Your white coats, your rock-pounding foreheads,
For our children lie there beyond us
In the still, foreign city of pain

Singing backward into the world
To those never seen before,

Old cool-handed doctors and young ones,
Capped girls bearing vessels of glucose,
Ginger ward boys, pan handlers, technicians,
Thieves, nightwalkers, truckers, and drunkards
Who must hear, not listening, them:
Them, crying: for they rise only unto

Those few who transcend themselves,
The superhuman tenderness of strangers.

All wheels; a man breathed fire,
Exhaling like a blowtorch down the road
And burnt the stripper's gown
Above her moving-barely feet.
A condemned train climbed from the earth
Up stilted nightlights zooming in a track.
I ambled along in that crowd

Between the gambling wheels
At carnival time with the others
Where the dodgem cars shuddered, sparking
On grillwire, each in his vehicle half
In control, half helplessly power-mad
As he was in the traffic that brought him.
No one blazed at me; then I saw

My mother and my father, he leaning
On a dog-chewed cane, she wrapped to the nose
In the fur of exhausted weasels.
I believed them buried miles back
In the country, in the faint sleep
Of the old, and had not thought to be
On this of all nights compelled

To follow where they led, not losing
Sight, with my heart enlarging whenever
I saw his crippled Stetson bob, saw her
With the teddy bear won on the waning
Whip of his right arm. They laughed;
She clung to him; then suddenly
The Wheel of wheels was turning

The colored night around.
They climbed aboard. My God, they rose
Above me, stopped themselves and swayed
Fifty feet up; he pointed

With his toothed cane, and took in
The whole Midway till they dropped,
Came down, went from me, came and went

Faster and faster, going up backward,
Cresting, out-topping, falling roundly.
From the crowd I watched them,
Their gold teeth flashing,
Until my eyes blurred with their riding
Lights, and I turned from the standing
To the moving mob, and went on:

Stepped upon sparking shocks
Of recognition when I saw my feet
Among the others, knowing them given,
Understanding the whirling impulse
From which I had been born,
The great gift of shaken lights,
The being wholly lifted with another,

All this having all and nothing
To do with me. Believers, I have seen
The wheel in the middle of the air
Where old age rises and laughs,
And on Lakewood Midway became
In five strides a kind of loving,
A mortal, a dutiful son.

From my great-grandmother on,
My family lies at Fairmount
In a small rigid house of Tate marble.
A Civil War general, a small one,
Rises into the air,
Always fifty feet away,
And there are always flowers
Surrounding him as he lifts
His sword and calls back over his shoulder
To his troops, none of which lie
Under the decent plots and polished stones
Of the civilian dead. Once I saw,
Or said I did, a lily wrapped
Around his tense hand and sword hilt.
An enormous glass-fronted hospital
Rises across the street, the traffic
Roars equally from all four sides,
And often, from a textile mill,
A teen-age girl wanders by,
Her head in a singing cloth
Still humming with bobbins and looms.
In summer, the hospital orderlies eat
Their lunches on the lawn
From wet-spotted brown paper bags,
While behind them the portioned glass
Of the hospital blindingly fits
The noon sun together:
A tremendous vertical blaze
From which one piece—off-center, northwest—
Is gone, where a window is open.
I have escaped from Fairmount
Through that square hole in the light,
Having found where that piece of the sun's
Stupendous puzzle resides. It is
Lying in the woods, in a small, unfenced
County graveyard in Alabama.
It is on an open book
Of cardboard and paper, a simulated Bible,

All white, like a giant bride's,
The only real pages the ones
The book opens to; light
From the trees is falling squarely
On the few large, hand-written words.
On a hunting trip I walked through
That place, far from all relatives
And wars, from bobbins and lilies and trucks.
Because of what I had seen,

I walked through the evergreen gates
Of the forest ranger's station,
And out to my car, and drove
To the county seat, and bought
My own secret grave-plot there
For thirty-seven dollars and a half.
A young deer, a spike buck, stood
Among the graves, slowly puzzling out
The not-quite-edible words
Of the book lying under
A panel of the sun forever
Missing from the noonlight of Fairmount.
I remember that, and sleep
Easier, seeing the animal head
Nuzzling the fragment of Scripture,
Browsing, before the first blotting rain
On the fragile book
Of the new dead, on words I take care,
Even in sleep, not to read,
Hoping for Genesis.

THE SHARK'S PARLOR

Memory: I can take my head and strike it on a wall   on Cumberland
    Island
Where the night tide came crawling under the stairs   came up the first
Two or three steps   and the cottage stood on poles all night
With the sea sprawled under it   as we dreamed of the great fin circling
Under the bedroom floor. In daylight there was my first brassy taste of
    beer
And Payton Ford and I came back from the Glynn County
    slaughterhouse
With a bucket of entrails and blood. We tied one end of a hawser
To a spindling porch pillar and rowed straight out of the house
Three hundred yards into the vast front yard of windless blue water
The rope outslithering its coil   the two-gallon jug stoppered and
    sealed
With wax   and a ten-foot chain leader   a drop-forged shark hook
    nestling.
We cast our blood on the waters   the land blood easily passing
For sea blood   and we sat in it for a moment with the stain spreading
Out from the boat   sat in a new radiance   in the pond of blood in
    the sea
Waiting for fins   waiting to spill our guts also in the glowing water.
We dumped the bucket, and baited the hook with a run-over collie pup.
    The jug
Bobbed, trying to shake off the sun as a dog would shake off the sea.
We rowed to the house   feeling the same water lift the boat a new way,
All the time seeing where we lived rise and dip with the oars.
We tied up and sat down in rocking chairs, one eye or the other
    responding
To the blue-eye wink of the jug. Payton got us a beer and we sat

All morning sat there with blood on our minds   the red mark out
In the harbor slowly failing us   then   the house groaned   the rope
Sprang out of the water   splinters flew   we leapt from our chairs
And grabbed the rope   hauled   did nothing   the house coming
    subtly
Apart   all around us   underfoot   boards beginning to sparkle
    like sand
With the glinting of the bright hidden parts of ten-year-old nails

Pulling out   the tarred poles we slept propped-up on   leaning to sea
As in land wind   crabs scuttling from under the floor   as we took
    turns about
Two more porch pillars   and looked out and saw   something
    a fish-flash
An almighty fin in trouble   a moiling of secret forces   a false start
Of water   a round wave growing: in the whole of Cumberland
    Sound the one ripple.
Payton took off without a word   I could not hold him either

But clung to the rope anyway: it was the whole house bending
Its nails that held whatever it was   coming in a little and like a fool
I took up the slack on my wrist. The rope drew gently   jerked   I lifted
Clean off the porch and hit the water   the same water it was in
I felt in blue blazing terror at the bottom of the stairs and scrambled
Back up looking desperately into the human house as deeply as I could
Stopping my gaze before it went out the wire screen of the back door
Stopped it on the thistled rattan   the rugs I lay on and read
On my mother's sewing basket with next winter's socks spilling from it
The flimsy vacation furniture   a bucktoothed picture of myself.
Payton came back with three men from a filling station   and glanced
    at me
Dripping water   inexplicable   then we all grabbed hold like a
    tug-of-war.

We were gaining a little   from us a cry went up   from everywhere
People came running. Behind us the house filled with men and boys.
On the third step from the sea I took my place   looking down the rope
Going into the ocean, humming and shaking off drops. A houseful
Of people put their backs into it   going up the steps from me
Into the living room   through the kitchen   down the back stairs
Up and over a hill of sand   across a dust road   and onto a raised field
Of dunes   we were gaining   the rope in my hands began to be wet
With deeper water   all other haulers retreated through the house
But Payton and I on the stairs   drawing hand over hand on our blood
Drawing into existence by the nose   a huge body   becoming
A hammerhead   rolling in beery shallows   and I began to let up
But the rope still strained behind me   the town had gone
Pulling-mad in our house: far away in a field of sand they struggled

206

They had turned their backs on the sea   bent double   some on their
    knees
The rope over their shoulders like a bag of gold   they strove for the
    ideal
Esso station across the scorched meadow   with the distant fish
    coming up
The front stairs   the sagging boards   still coming in   up   taking
Another step   toward the empty house   where the rope stood
    straining
By itself through the rooms   in the middle of the air. "Pass the word,"
Payton said, and I screamed it: "Let up, good God, let up!"   to no one
    there.
The shark flopped on the porch, grating with salt-sand   driving
    back in
The nails he had pulled out   coughing chunks of his formless blood.
The screen door banged and tore off   he scrambled on his tail   slid
Curved   did a thing from another world   and was out of his
    element and in
Our vacation paradise   cutting all four legs from under the dinner
    table
With one deep-water move   he unwove the rugs in a moment
    throwing pints
Of blood over everything we owned   knocked the buck teeth out of
    my picture
His odd head full of crushed jelly-glass splinters and radio tubes
    thrashing
Among the pages of fan magazines   all the movie stars drenched in
    sea-blood.
Each time we thought he was dead   he struggled back and smashed
One more thing   in all coming back to die   three or four more
    times after death.
At last we got him out   log-rolling him   greasing his sandpaper skin
With lard to slide him   pulling on his chained lips as the tide came
Tumbled him down the steps as the first night wave went under the
    floor.
He drifted off   head back   belly white as the moon. What could I
    do but buy
That house   for the one black mark still there   against death   a
    forehead-

toucher in the room he circles beneath   and has been invited to
    wreck?
Blood hard as iron on the wall   black with time   still bloodlike
Can be touched whenever the brow is drunk enough: all changes:
    Memory:
Something like three-dimensional dancing in the limbs   with age
Feeling more in two worlds than one   in all worlds the growing
    encounters.

III

PURSUIT FROM UNDER

Often, in these blue meadows,
I hear what passes for the bark of seals

And on August week ends the cold of a personal ice age
Comes up through my bare feet
Which are trying to walk like a boy's again
So that nothing on earth can have changed
On the ground where I was raised.

The dark grass here is like
The pads of mukluks going on and on

Because I once burned kerosene to read
Myself near the North Pole
In the journal of Arctic explorers
Found, years after death, preserved
In a tent, part of whose canvas they had eaten

Before the last entry.
All over my father's land

The seal holes sigh like an organ,
And one entry carries more terror
Than the blank page that signified death
In 1912, on the icecap.
It says that, under the ice,

The killer whale darts and distorts,
Cut down by the flawing glass

To a weasel's shadow,
And when, through his ceiling, he sees
Anything darker than snow

He falls away
To gather more and more force

From the iron depths of cold water,
His shadow dwindling

Almost to nothing at all, then charges
Straight up, looms up at the ice and smashes
Into it with his forehead
To splinter the roof, to isolate seal or man
On a drifting piece of the floe

Which he can overturn.
If you run, he will follow you

Under the frozen pane,
Turning as you do, zigzagging,
And at the most uncertain of your ground
Will shatter through, and lean,
And breathe frankly in your face

An enormous breath smelling of fish.
With the stale lungs staining your air

You know the unsaid recognition
Of which the explorers died:
They had been given an image
Of how the downed dead pursue us.
They knew, as they starved to death,

That not only in the snow
But in the family field

The small shadow moves,
And under bare feet in the summer:
That somewhere the turf will heave,
And the outraged breath of the dead,
So long held, will form

Unbreathably around the living.
The cows low oddly here

As I pass, a small bidden shape
Going with me, trembling like foxfire
Under my heels and their hooves.
I shall write this by kerosene,
Pitch a tent in the pasture, and starve.

FOX BLOOD

Blood blister over my thumb-moon
Rising, under clear still plastic
Still rising strongly, on the rise
Of unleashed dog-sounds: sound broke,
Log opened. Moon rose

Clear bright. Dark homeland
Peeled backward, scrambling its vines.
Stream showed, scent paled
In the spray of mountain-cold water.
The smell dogs followed

In the bush-thorns hung like a scarf,
The silver sharp creek
Cut; off yonder, fox feet
Went printing into the dark: *there,*
In the other wood,

The uncornered animal's, running
Is half floating off
Upon instinct. Sails spread, fox wings
Lift him alive over gullies,
Hair tips all over him lightly

Touched with the moon's red silver,
Back-hearing around
The stream of his body the tongue of hounds
Feather him. In his own animal sun
Made of human moonlight,

He flies like a bolt running home,
Whose passage kills the current in the river,
Whose track through the cornfield shakes
The symmetry from the rows.
Once shot, he dives through a bush

And disappears into air.
That is the bush my hand
Went deeply through as I followed.
Like a wild hammer blazed my right thumb
In the flashlight and moonlight

And dried to one drop
Of fox blood I nail-polished in,
That lopsided animal sun
Over the nearly buried
Or rising human half-moon,

My glassed skin halfmooning wrongly.
Between them, the logging road, the stopped
Stream, the disappearance into
The one bush's common, foreseen
Superhuman door:

All this where I nailed it,
With my wife's nailbrush, on my finger,
To keep, not under, but over
My thumb, a hammering day-and-night sign
Of that country.

FATHERS AND SONS

I. THE SECOND SLEEP

Curled, too much curled, he was sleeping

In a chair too small for him, a restless chair
That held no place for his arms;

In his sleep he grew legs to replace them

As his father liftingly strained
And carried him to the next room.

All the time he settled away

A gentle man looked upon him
And then walked out of the house

And started his evergreen car.

Terrific impact, none his,
Killed him three blocks to the north.

In his second sleep the boy heard

The reared-up tearing of metal
Where a glassed-in face leapt and broke,

But to him it was something else,

An animal clash, a shock of resolving antlers,
And slept on, deeper and deeper

Into the mating season.

The next room filled with women; his nostrils
Flared, his eyes grew wide

And shot with blood under eyelids.

Brow lowered in strife, he stamped
In the laurel thicket, a herd of does

Trembling around him. Into the rhododendron

His rival faded like rain.
He stared around wildly, head down.

In the undying green, they woke him.

    II. THE AURA
He used to wake to him
With a sense of music coming
Along with a body in movement.
It swayed with the motion of a hip
Rolling into the bathroom,
And, lying in bed in the winter dark

Of fathers, he heard rock-and-roll
Closed off while water ran through it,
Then the door opening, music
Opening, strolling down the hall,
Bad music moving all over
The house, electric guitars that followed

Some body around. It was his son,
With his portable radio always
At his belt, leaning over, adjusting the dial
For disc jockeys. That would be
The Skimmers, and that the Last
Survivors, moaning afar in the kitchen,

Who moved when the living moved.
He could hear him coming
From far away, every dawn,
And now the sound still coming
From everywhere is grief,
Unstoppable. At the beginning

Of his teens, his last year
Of bicycles, the wild
Music, traveling through the suburbs
From junior high, was broken on the road.
But it leapt everywhere
Into odd places: from every angle

It does not cease to be heard, the aura
Surrounding his son. He cannot hear it early
In the morning, unless he turns on his radio
By the bed, or leaves it on all night,
But in supermarkets it comes
Forth from the walls; it glances

From plate glass in department stores,
And he moves within his boy's
Chosen sounds: in cars, theatres,
In filling stations, in beer joints
Where he sits as though in the next phase
His son would have lived, hearing voices

Giving prizes for naming of tunes, those stations
Never off the air. He sits still
Wherever he is, as though caught
With music on him, or as if he were
About to be given it somewhere
In the region of the stomach:

That sound is the same, and yet not—
There is too much steadiness in it: none
Is carried rightly, none wavers
With the motion of adolescent walking, none
Lumbers as it should. Still, it is there
In trios of girls, in fake folk singers

From Brooklyn, and he enters, anywhere,
His son's life without the waking-
to-it, the irreplaceable motion
Of a body. Bongoes. Steel
Guitars. A precious cheapness
He would have grown out of. Something. Music.

SLED BURIAL, DREAM CEREMONY

While the south rains, the north
Is snowing, and the dead southerner
Is taken there. He lies with the top of his casket
Open, his hair combed, the particles in the air
Changing to other things. The train stops

In a small furry village, and men in flap-eared caps
And others with women's scarves tied around their heads
And business hats over those, unload him,
And one of them reaches inside the coffin and places
The southerner's hand at the center

Of his dead breast. They load him onto a sled,
An old-fashioned sled with high-curled runners,
Drawn by horses with bells, and begin
To walk out of town, past dull red barns
Inching closer to the road as it snows

Harder, past an army of gunny-sacked bushes,
Past horses with flakes in the hollows of their sway-backs,
Past round faces drawn by children
On kitchen windows, all shedding basic-shaped tears.
The coffin top still is wide open;

His dead eyes stare through his lids,
Not fooled that the snow is cotton. The woods fall
Slowly off all of them, until they are walking
Between rigid little houses of ice-fishers
On a plain which is a great plain of water

Until the last rabbit track fails, and they are
At the center. They take axes, shovels, mattocks,

218

Dig the snow away, and saw the ice in the form
Of his coffin, lifting the slab like a door
Without hinges. The snow creaks under the sled

As they unload him like hay, holding his weight by ropes.
Sensing an unwanted freedom, a fish
Slides by, under the hole leading up through the snow
To nothing, and is gone. The coffin's shadow
Is white, and they stand there, gunny-sacked bushes,

Summoned from village sleep into someone else's dream
Of death, and let him down, still seeing the flakes in the air
At the place they are born of pure shadow
Like his dead eyelids, rocking for a moment like a boat
On utter foreignness, before he fills and sails down.

GAMECOCK

Fear, jealousy and murder are the same
When they put on their long reddish feathers,
Their shawl neck and moccasin head
In a tree bearing levels of women.
There is yet no thread

Of light, and his scabbed feet tighten,
Holding sleep as though it were lockjaw,
His feathers damp, his eyes crazed
And cracked like the eyes
Of a chicken head cut off or wrung-necked

While he waits for the sun's only cry
All night building up in his throat
To leap out and turn the day red,
To tumble his hens from the pine tree,
And then will go down, his hackles

Up, looking everywhere for the other
Cock who could not be there,
Head ruffed and sullenly stepping
As upon his best human-curved steel:
He is like any fierce

Old man in a terminal ward:
There is the same look of waiting
That the sun prepares itself for;
The enraged, surviving-
another-day blood,

And from him at dawn comes the same
Cry that the world cannot stop.
In all the great building's blue windows
The sun gains strength; on all floors, women
Awaken—wives, nurses, sisters and daughters—

And he lies back, his eyes filmed, unappeased,
As all of them, clucking, pillow-patting,
Come to help his best savagery blaze, doomed, dead-
game, demanding, unreasonably
Battling to the death for what is his.

THE NIGHT POOL

There is this other element that shines
At night near human dwellings, glows like wool
From the sides of itself, far down:

From the deep end of heated water
I am moving toward her, first swimming,
Then touching my light feet to the floor,

Rising like steam from the surface
To take her in my arms, beneath the one window
Still giving off unsleeping light.

There is this other element, it being late
Enough, and in it I lift her, and can carry
Her over any threshold in the world,

Into any of these houses, apartments,
Her shoulders streaming, or above them
Into the mythical palaces. Her body lies

In my arms like a child's, not drowned,
Not drowned, and I float with her off
My feet. We are here; we move differently,

Sustained, closer together, not weighing
On ourselves or on each other, not near fish
Or anything but light, the one human light

From above that we lie in, breathing
Its precious abandoned gold. We rise out
Into our frozen land-bodies, and her lips

Turn blue, sealed against me. What I can do
In the unforgivable cold, in the least
Sustaining of all brute worlds, is to say

Nothing, not ask forgiveness, but only
Give her all that in my condition
I own, wrap her in many towels.

It wounded well—one time and
A half: once with instant blood and again
Reinfecting blackly, years later. Now all
    Is calm at the heel of my hand

    Where I grabbed, in a bellied-
in airplane, and caught the dark glass
Offered once in a lifetime by
    The brittle tachometer.

    Moons by the thousands
Have risen in all that time; I hold
The healed half-moon of that night.
    I tell it to shine as still

    As it can in the temperate flesh
That never since has balled into a fist,
To hover on nylon guitar strings
    Like the folk-moon itself;

    I tell it to burn like a poison
When my two children threaten themselves,
Wall-walking, or off the deep end
    Of a county swimming pool,

    And with thousands of moons
Coming over me year after year,
I lie with it well under cover,
    The war of the millions,

    Through glass ground under
Heel twenty-one years ago
Concentrating its light on my hand,
    Small, but with world-fury.

MANGHAM

Somewhere between bells the right angles staggered
And Mangham poised, sensing thunder,
Something crookèd in the straight lines of his brain.
Chalk dust rose from his shoulders, lost more
Weight, settled upward. The blackboard altered
Its screech, and the teeth of the children were set
On edge.

Above our doped heads the ceiling whitened
As the part in Mr. Mangham's hair
Lost its way; a gray lock fell;
Behind him as he turned, the Law
Of Cosines. He pressed the middle of his brow
With a handkerchief, looking at all of us
As he stepped

Quickly out of the room. In the center
Of the high school a sound arose from us,
A hive sound, amazing, increasing. I tore up my note
To Serena Hill, and leaned and spoke
Boldly to her in person. At the threshold
Mr. Mangham appeared with a handkerchief
Full of lumps;

He had raided the lunchroom icebox, and held
A knotted cloth full of soupy cubes
Dripping down his gray face: held it
Left-handed, lifted his good
Right arm. The signs appeared again,
The blackboard filled
With crazy proofs,

Lines wavering on the powdery blackness,
The dark night of the adolescent mind,
Conceiving drunken constellations,
Equilateral triangles, others of thirty-
sixty-ninety degrees, traced by a seismograph,

All figures melting from the ice-
colors of his chalk.

It should be in a tent in the desert
That I remember Mangham's last day
In that class, for his cracked voice was speaking
Of perfection, sphere-music,
Through the stroke that blazed in his mind
As our hive toned down
And Pythagoras howled

For more ice: it should be in contemplative sand
Or in a corner that I ought to sit
On a high stool, Mangham's age now,
On my head a conical hat, a dunce cap
Covered with moons and stars and jagged bands
Of brain-lightning, the ceiling above me
White with the chalk motes

Of stars from my shoulders, the night blazoned
With the angles of galaxies forming
To a silent music's accords,
Proving once and for all that I have no head
For figures, but knowing that that did not stop
Mangham for one freezing minute
Of his death

From explaining for my own good, from the good
Side of his face, while the other
Mixed unfelt sweat and ice water, what I never
Could get to save my soul: those things that, once
Established, cannot be changed by angels,
Devils, lightning, ice or indifference:
Identities! Identities!

ANGINA

That one who is the dreamer lies mostly in her left arm,
Where the pain shows first,
Tuned in on the inmost heart,
Never escaping. On the blue, bodied mound of chenille,
That limb lies still.
Death in the heart must be calm,

Must not look suddenly, but catch the windowframed squirrel
In a mild blue corner
Of an eye staring straight at the ceiling
And hold him there.
Cornered also, the oak tree moves
All the ruffled green way toward itself

Around the squirrel thinking of the sun
As small boys and girls tiptoe in
Overawed by their existence,
For courtly doctors long dead
Have told her that to bear children
Was to die, and they are the healthy issue

Of four of those. Oh, beside that room the oak leaves
Burn out their green in an instant, renew it all
From the roots when the wind stops.
All afternoon she dreams of letters
To disc jockeys, requesting the "old songs,"
The songs of the nineties, when she married, and caught

With her first child rheumatic fever.
Existence is family: sometime,
Inadequate ghosts round the bed,
But mostly voices, low voices of serious drunkards
Coming in with the night light on
And the pink radio turned down;

She hears them ruin themselves
On the rain-weeping wires, the bearing-everything poles,
Then dozes, not knowing sleeping from dying—

It is day. Limbs stiffen when the heart beats
Wrongly. Her left arm tingles,
The squirrel's eye blazes up, the telephone rings,

Her children and her children's children fail
In school, marriage, abstinence, business.
But when I think of love
With the best of myself—that odd power—
I think of riding, by chairlift,
Up a staircase burning with dust

In the afternoon sun slanted also
Like stairs without steps
To a room where an old woman lies
Who can stand on her own two feet
Only six strange hours every month:
Where such a still one lies smiling

And takes her appalling risks
In absolute calm, helped only by the most
Helplessly bad music in the world, where death,
A chastened, respectful presence
Forced by years of excessive quiet
To be stiller than wallpaper roses,

Waits, twined in the roses, saying slowly
To itself, as sprier and sprier
Generations of disc jockeys chatter,
I must be still and not worry,
Not worry, not worry, to hold
My peace, my poor place, my own.

DUST

Lying at home
Anywhere   it can change not only the color
But the shape of the finger that runs along it   leaving a trail
That disappears from the earth; nothing can follow
Where that hand has walked and withdrawn.
And I have lain in bed at home and watched

Through a haze
Of afternoon liquor   the sun come down through it
Dropping off at the window sill from which the dust has risen
With no voice   the voices of children   to spin
In a stunned silence   the individual motes
All with a shape apiece   wool fragments

Small segments
Of rope tricks   spirochetes boring into the very
Body of light   and if you move your hand through their air
They dip   weave   then assume in the altered brightness
The places they have had, and all
Their wandering. Wherever it is,

It rises;
The place stands up and whirls   as in valleys
Of Arizona   where the world-armies of dust gather in sleeping
Hordes. I have seen them walking
Nearly out of the world   on a crazed foot
Spinning the ground beneath them

Into chaos.
These are dust devils, and in that sunny room
With the shape of their motes unmassed   not given a desert
I have closed my eyes and changed them into forms
Of fire   the dying's vision
Of incandescent worms:

For moment
After moment have lain as though whirling
Toward myself from the grains of the earth   in a cone

228

Of sunlight   massing my forces
To live in time   drawn into a shape
Of dust   and in that place

A woman
Came from my spinning side. There we lay
And stared at the ceiling of our house   at the extra motes
That danced about the raising of our hands
Unable to get in-
to a human form at this time

But ready
For children we might raise and call our own,
Teach to sing   to sweep the sills   to lift their hands
And make the dust dance in the air
Like bodies: ready:
Ready, always, for the next.

THE FIEND

He has only to pass by a tree   moodily walking   head down
A worried accountant   not with it   and he is swarming
He is gliding up the underside light of leaves   upfloating
In a seersucker suit   passing window after window of her building.
He finds her at last, chewing gum   talking on the telephone.
The wind sways him softly   comfortably sighing   she must bathe
Or sleep.   She gets up, and he follows her along the branch
Into another room.   She stands there for a moment   and the
    teddy bear
On the bed feels its guts spin as she takes it by the leg and tosses
It off.   She touches one button at her throat, and rigor mortis
Slithers into his pockets, making everything there—keys, pen
and secret love—stand up.   He brings from those depths the knife
And flicks it open   it glints on the moon one time   carries
Through the dead walls   making a wormy static on the TV screen.
He parts the swarm of gnats that live excitedly at this perilous level
Parts the rarefied light high windows give out into inhabited trees
Opens his lower body to the moon.   This night the apartments are
    sinking

To ground level   burying their sleepers in the soil   burying all floors
But the one where a sullen shopgirl gets ready to take a shower,
Her hair in rigid curlers, and the rest.   When she gives up
Her aqua terry-cloth robe the wind quits in mid-tree   the birds
Freeze to their perches round his head   a purely human light
Comes out of a one-man oak   around her an energy field   she stands
Rooted   not turning to anything else   then begins to move like a saint
Her stressed nipples rising like things about to crawl off her   as he gets
A hold on himself.   With that clasp she changes   senses   something

Some breath through the fragile walls   some all-seeing eye
Of God   some touch that enfolds her body   some hand come up
    out of roots
That carries her as she moves   swaying   at this rare height.
    She wraps
The curtain around her and streams.   The room fades.   Then coming
Forth magnificently   the window blurred from within   she moves
    in a cloud

Chamber   the tree in the oak currents sailing   in clear air keeping
     pace
With her white breathless closet—he sees her mistily part her lips
As if singing to him,come up from river-fog   almost hears her as if
She sang alone in a cloud   its warmed light streaming into his branches
Out through the gauze glass of the window.   She takes off her
     bathing cap
The tree with him ascending   himself and the birds all moving
In darkness together   crumbling the bark in their claws.
By this time he holds in his awkward, subtle limbs the limbs

Of a hundred understanding trees.   He has learned what a plant is like
When it moves near a human habitation   moving closer the later it is
Unfurling its leaves near bedrooms   still keeping its wilderness life
Twigs covering his body with only one way out   for his eyes into
     inner light
Of a chosen window   living with them night after night   watching
Watching with them at times their favorite TV shows   learning—
Though now and then he hears a faint sound: gunshot, bombing,
Building-fall—how to read lips: the lips of laconic cowboys
Bank robbers   old and young doctors tense-faced   gesturing savagely
In wards and corridors   like reading the lips of the dead

The lips of men interrupting the program at the wrong time
To sell you a good used car on the Night Owl Show   men silently
     reporting
The news out the window.   But the living as well, three-dimensioned,
Silent as the small gray dead, must sleep at last   must save their lives
By taking off their clothes. It is his beholding that saves them:
God help the dweller in windowless basements   the one obsessed
With drawing curtains this night. At three o'clock in the morning
He descends   a medium-sized shadow   while that one sleeps and
     turns
In her high bed in loss   as he goes limb by limb   quietly down
The trunk with one lighted side. Ground upon which he could not
     explain
His presence he walks with toes uncurled from branches, his
     bird-movements
Dying hard. At the sidewalk he changes   gains weight   a solid citizen

Once more. At apartments there is less danger from dogs, but he has
For those a super-quiet hand   a hand to calm sparrows and rivers,
And watchdogs in half-tended bushes lie with him watching their
    women
Undress   the dog's honest eyes and the man's the same pure beast's
Comprehending the same essentials. Not one of these beheld would
    ever give
Him a second look   but he gives them all a first look that goes
On and on   conferring immortality while it lasts   while the
    suburb's leaves
Hold still enough   while whatever dog he has with him holds its breath
Yet seems to thick-pant   impatient as he with the indifferent men
Drifting in and out of the rooms   or staying on, too tired to move
Reading the sports page   dozing   plainly unworthy   for what
    women want
Dwells in bushes and trees: what they want is to look outward,

To look with the light streaming into the April limbs   to stand
    straighter
While their husbands' lips dry out   feeling that something is there
That could dwell in no earthly house: that in poplar trees or beneath
The warped roundabout of the clothesline   in the sordid disorder
Of communal backyards   some being is there in the shrubs
Sitting comfortably on a child's striped rubber ball filled with rainwater
Muffling his glasses with a small studious hand against a sudden
Flash of houselight from within   or flash from himself   a needle's eye
Uncontrollable   blaze of uncompromised being. Ah, the lingerie
Hung in the bathroom! The domestic motions of single girls living
    together
A plump girl girding her loins against her moon-summoned blood:
In that moon he stands   the only male lit by it, covered with
    leaf-shapes.
He coughs, and the smallest root responds   and in his lust he is set
By the wind in motion. That movement can restore the green eyes
Of middle age   looking   renewed   through the qualified light
Not quite reaching him where he stands again on the usual branch
Of his oldest love   his tie not loosened   a plastic shield
In his breast pocket full of pencils and ballpoint pens given him by
    salesmen

His hat correctly placed to shade his eyes   a natural gambler's tilt
And in summer wears an eyeshade   a straw hat Caribbean style.
In some guise or other he is near them when they are weeping without
     sound
When the teen-age son has quit school   when the girl has broken up
With the basketball star   when the banker walks out on his wife.
He sees mothers counsel desperately with pulsing girls face down
On beds full of overstuffed beasts   sees men dress as women
In ante-bellum costumes with bonnets   sees doctors come, looking
     oddly
Like himself   though inside the houses   worming a medical arm
Up under the cringing covers   sees children put angrily to bed
Sees one told an invisible fairy story   with lips moving silently as his
Are also moving   the book's few pages bright. It will take years
But at last he will shed his leaves   burn his roots   give up
Invisibility   will step out   will make himself known to the one
He cannot see loosen her blouse   take off luxuriously   with lips
Compressed against her mouth-stain   her dress   her stockings
Her magic underwear.   To that one he will come   up frustrated pines
Down alleys   through window blinds   blind windows   kitchen doors
On summer evenings. It will be something small that sets him off:
Perhaps a pair of lace pants on a clothesline   gradually losing
Water to the sun   filling out in the warm light with a well-rounded
Feminine wind as he watches   having spent so many sleepless nights
Because of her   because of her hand on a shade always coming down
In his face   not leaving even a shadow stripped naked upon the
     brown paper
Waiting for her now in a green outdated car with a final declaration
Of love   pretending to read   and when she comes and takes down
Her pants, he will casually follow her in   like a door-to-door salesman
The godlike movement of trees stiffening with him   the light
Of a hundred favored windows   gone wrong somewhere in his glasses
Where his knocked-off panama hat was   in his painfully vanishing
     hair.

IV

SLAVE QUARTERS

In the great place the great house is gone from   in the sun
Room, near the kitchen of air   I look across at low walls
Of slave quarters, and feel my imagining loins

Rise with the madness of Owners
To take off the Master's white clothes
And slide all the way into moonlight
Two hundred years old with this moon.
Let me go,

Ablaze with my old me-
scent, in moonlight made by the mind
From the dusk sun, in the yard where my dogs would smell
For once what I totally am,
Flaming up in their brains as the Master
They but dimly had sensed through my clothes:
Let me stand as though moving

At midnight, now at the instant of sundown
When the wind turns

From sea wind to land, and the marsh grass
Hovers, changing direction:
                              there was this house
That fell before I got out. I can pull
It over me where I stand, up from the earth,
Back out of the shells
Of the sea:
            become with the change of this air
A coastal islander, proud of his grounds,
His dogs, his spinet
From Savannah, his pale daughters,
His war with the sawgrass, pushed back into
The sea it crawled from. Nearer dark, unseen,

I can begin to dance
Inside my gabardine suit
As though I had left my silk nightshirt

In the hall of mahogany, and crept
To slave quarters to live out
The secret legend of Owners. Ah, stand up,
Blond loins, another
Love is possible! My thin wife would be sleeping
Or would not mention my absence:

                  the moonlight

On these rocks can be picked like cotton
By a crazed Owner dancing-mad
With the secret repossession of his body

Phosphorescent and mindless, shedding
Blond-headed shadow on the sand,
Hounds pressing in their sleep
Around him, smelling his footblood
On the strange ground that lies between skins
With the roof blowing off slave quarters
To let the moon in burning
The years away
In just that corner where crabgrass proves it lives
Outside of time.
Who seeks the other color of his body,
His loins giving off a frail light
On the dark lively shipwreck of grass   sees
Water live where
The half-moon touches,
The moon made whole in one wave
Very far from the silent piano   the copy of Walter Scott
Closed on its thin-papered battles
Where his daughter practiced, decorum preventing the one
Bead of sweat in all that lace   collected at her throat
From breaking and humanly running
Over Mozart's unmortal keys—

                              I come past
A sand crab pacing sideways   his eyes out
On stalks   the bug-eyed vision of fiddler
Crabs sneaking a light on the run
From the split moon   holding in it a white man stepping
Down the road of clamshells and cotton   his eyes out
On stems   the tops of the sugar
Cane soaring   the sawgrass walking:
                                   I come past
The stale pools left
Over from high tide   where the crab in the night sand
Is basting himself with his claws   moving ripples outward
Feasting on brightness
                        and above
A gull also crabs slowly,
Tacks, jibes   then turning the corner
Of wind, receives himself like a brother
As he glides down upon his reflection:

My body has a color not yet freed:
In that ruined house let me throw
Obsessive gentility off;
Let Africa rise upon me like a man
Whose instincts are delivered from their chains
Where they lay close-packed and wide-eyed
In muslin sheets
As though in the miserly holding
Of too many breaths by one ship.   Now

Worked in silver   their work lies all
Around me   the fields dissolving
Into the sea   and   not on a horse
I stoop to the soil   working
Gathering   moving to the rhythm of a music
That has crossed the ocean in chains

In the grass the great singing void of slave

Labor about me   the moonlight bringing
Sweat out of my back as though the sun

Changed skins upon me   some other
Man moving near me on horseback   whom I look in the eyes
Once a day:
        there in that corner

Her bed turned to grass. Unsheltered by these walls
The outside fields form slowly
Anew, in a kind of barrelling blowing,
Bend in all the right places   as faintly Michael rows
The boat ashore   his spiritual lungs
Entirely filling the sail.   How take on the guilt

Of slavers? How shudder like one who made
Money from buying a people
To work as ghosts
In this blowing solitude?
I only stand here upon shells   dressed poorly
For nakedness   poorly
For the dark wrecked hovel of rebirth

Picking my way in thought
To the black room
Where starlight blows off the roof
And the great beasts that came in the minds
Of the first slaves, stand at the door, asking
For death, asking to be
Forgotten: the sadness of elephants
The visionary pain in the heads
Of incredibly poisonous snakes
Lion   wildebeest   giraffe   all purchased also
When one wished only
Labor
      those beasts becoming
For the white man the animals of Eden
Emblems of sexual treasure   all beasts attending
Me now   my dreamed dogs snarling at the shades
Of eland and cheetah
On the dispossessed ground where I dance
In my clothes beyond movement:

In nine months she would lie
With a knife between her teeth to cut the pain
Of bearing
A child who belongs in no world   my hair in that boy
Turned black   my skin
Darkened by half   his, lightened
By that half exactly   the beasts of Africa reduced
To cave shadows flickering on his brow
As I think of him: a child would rise from that place
With half my skin.   He could for an instant
Of every day   when the wind turns   look
Me in the eyes.   What do you feel when passing

Your blood beyond death
To another in secret: into
Another who takes your features   and adds
A misplaced Africa to them,
Changing them forever
As they must live?   What happens
To you, when such a one bears
You after your death into rings
Of battling light   a heavyweight champion
Through the swirling glass of four doors,
In epauletted coats   into places
Where you learn to wait
On tables   into sitting in all-night cages
Of parking lots   into raising
A sun-sided hammer in a gang
Of men on a tar road working
Until the crickets give up?
What happens when the sun goes down

And the white man's loins still stir
In a house of air   still draw him toward
Slave quarters? When Michael's voice is heard
Bending the sail like grass,
The real moon begins to come
Apart on the water
And two hundred years are turned back
On with the headlights of a car?

238

When you learn that there is no hatred
Like love in the eyes
Of a wholly owned face?   When you think of what
It would be like   what it has been
What it is to look once a day
Into an only
Son's brown, waiting, wholly possessed
Amazing eyes, and not
Acknowledge, but own?

Falling

To Monroe Spears

I

REINCARNATION (II)

—the white thing was so white, its
    wings
so wide, and in those for ever exiled
    waters
                 —MELVILLE

As apparitional as sails that cross
Some page of figures to be filed
    away
                 —HART CRANE

One can do   one begins to   one can only

Circle   eyes wide with fearing the spirit

Of weight   as though to be born   to awaken to what one is
Were to be carried   passed out
With enormous cushions of air under the arms
Straight up   the head growing stranger
And released between wings near an iceberg

It is too much to ask   to ask
For   under the white mild sun
On that huge frozen point to move

As one is so easily doing

Boring into it with one's new
born excessive eye   after a long
Half-sleeping self-doubting voyage   until
The unbased mountain falters
Turns over like a whale   one screams for the first time

With a wordless voice   swings over
The berg's last treasured bubble
Straightens   wings trembling   RIDING!

Rises into a new South

Sensitive current   checks each wing
It is living there
                    and starts out.

There is then this night
Crawling slowly in under one wing
This night of all nights
Aloft   a night five thousand feet up
Where he soars among the as-yet-unnamed
The billion unmentionable stars
Each in its right relation
To his course   he shivers   changes his heading
Slightly   feels the heavenly bodies
Shake   alter   line up in the right conjunction
For mating   for the plunge
Toward the egg   he soars   borne toward his offspring

By the Dragon balanced exactly
Again the Lion   the sense of the galaxies
Right from moment to moment
Drawing slowly for him a Great
Circle   all the stars in the sky
Embued with the miracle of
The single human Christmas one
Conjoining to stand now over
A rocky island ten thousand
Miles of water away.
                         With a cold new heart
With celestial feathered crutches
A "new start" like a Freudian dream
Of a new start   he hurtles as if motionless
All the air in the upper world
Splitting apart on his lips.

Sleep   *wingless* —NO!
The stars appear, rimmed with red
Space under his breastbone maintains
Itself   he sighs like a man

Between his cambered wings
Letting down now   curving around
Into the wind   slowly toward
Any wave   that—
That one.   He folds his wings and moves
With the mid-Pacific
Carried for miles in no particular direction
On a single wave   a wandering hill
Surging softly along in a powerful
Long-lost phosphorous seethe   folded in those wings
Those ultimate wings   home is like   home is
A folding of wings   Mother
Something whispers   one eye opens   a star shifts
Does not fall   from the eye of the Swan   he dreams

He sees the Southern Cross
Painfully over the horizon   drawing itself
Together   inching
Higher each night of the world   thorn
Points   tilted   he watches   not to be taken in
By the False Cross   as in   in
Another life   not taken

Knowing the true south rises
In a better make of cross   smaller   compact
And where its lights must appear.
Just after midnight he rises
And goes for it   joy with him
Springing out of the water
Disguised as wind   he checks each feather
As the stars burn out   waiting
Taking his course on faith until
The east begins
To pulse with unstoppable light.
Now darkness and dawn melt exactly
Together on one indifferent rill
Which sinks and is
Another   he lives

In renewed light, utterly alone!

In five days there is one ship
Dragging its small chewed off-white
Of ship-water   one candle in a too-human cabin
One vessel moving embedded
In its blue endurable country

Water warms   thereafter it is not
That the sea begins to tinge
Like a vast, laid smoke
But that he closes his eyes and feels himself
Turning whiter and whiter   upheld

At his whitest it is

Midnight   the equator   the center of the world
He sneaks across   afire
With himself   the stars change all their figures
Reach toward him   closer
And now begin to flow
Into his cracked-open mouth   down his throat
A string of lights   emblems   patterns of fire   all
Directions   myths   Hydras
Centaurs   Wolves   Virgins
Eating them all   eating
The void   possessing
Music   order   repose
Hovering   moving on his armbones   crawling
On warm air   covering the whole ocean   the sea deadens
He dulls   new constellations pale off
Him   unmapped roads open out of his breast
Beyond the sick feeling
Of those whose arms drag at treasures   it is like

Roosting   like holding one's arms out
In a clean nightshirt   a good dream   it is all
Instinct   he thinks   I have been born
This way.
                    Goes on
His small head holding
It all   the continents firmly fixed

246

By his gaze   five new ships turned
Rusty by his rich shadow.
His seamless shoulders of dawn-gold
Open   he opens
Them wider   an inch wider and he would

Trees   voices   white garments   meadows
Fail   under him again are
Mullet believing their freedom
Is to go anywhere they like in their collected shape
The form of an unthrown net
With no net anywhere near them.
Of these he eats.
                    Taking off again
He rocks forward three more days
Twenty-four hours a day
Balancing without thinking—
In doubt, he opens his bill
And vastness adjusts him
He trims his shoulders and planes   up

Up   stalls

In midocean   falls off
Comes down in a long, unbeheld
Curve that draws him deep into

                              evening

Incredible pasture.

The Cross is up.   Looking in through its four panes
He sees something   a clean desk-top
Papers shuffled   hears
Something   a bird word
A too-human word   a word
That should have been somewhere spoken
That now can be frankly said
With long stiff lips into
The center of the Southern Cross
A word enabling one to fly

Out the window of office buildings
Lifts up on wings of its own
To say itself over and over   sails on
Under the unowned stars   sails as if walking
Out the window
That is what I said
That is what I should   that is

Dawn.   Panic   one moment of thinking
Himself in the hell of thumbs   once more   a man
Disguised in these wings   alone   No   again
He thinks   I am here   I have been born
This way   raised up from   raised up in
Myself   my soul
Undivided at last   thrown slowly forward
Toward an unmanned island.

Day overcomes   night comes over
Day with day already

Coming behind it   the sun halved in the east
The moon pressing feathers together.
Who thinks his bones are light
Enough, should try it   it is for everyone
He thinks   the world is for everything born—
I always had
These wings   buried deep in my back:
There is a wing-growing motion
Half-alive in every creature.

Comes down   skims for fifty miles
All afternoon lies skimming
His white shadow burning his breast
The flying-fish darting before him
In and out of the ash-film glaze

Or "because it is there"   into almighty cloud

In rain crying hoarsely
No place to go except

Forward into water in the eyes
Tons of water falling on the back
For hours   no sight   no insight
Beating up   trying
To rise above it   not knowing which way
Is up   no stars   crying
Home   fire   windows   for God
Sake   beating down   up   up-down
No help   streaming   another
Death   vertigo   falling
Upward   mother   God   country
Then seizing one grain of water in his mouth
Glides forward   heavy with cloud
Enveloped   gigantic   blazing with St. Elmo's
Fire   alone at the heart
Of rain   pure bird   heaving up   going

Up from that
                    and from that

Finally breaking

Out   where the sun is violently shining

On the useless enormous ploughland
Of cloud   then up
From just above it   up
Reducing the clouds more and more
To the color of their own defeat
The beauty of history   forgotten bird-
kingdoms packed in batting
The soft country   the endless fields
Raining away beneath him   to be dead
In one life is to enter
Another   to break out   to rise above   the clouds
Fail   pull back their rain

Dissolve.   All the basic blue beneath
Comes back, tattering through. He cries out
As at sight of home   a last human face

In a mirror dazzles   he reaches
Glides off on one wing   stretching himself wider
Floats into night   dark follows
At his pace
                    the stars' threads all connect
On him   and, each in its place, the islands
Rise   small form of beaches

Treeless   tons of guano   eggshells
Of generations
                    down
                              circling

Mistrusting

The land   coming in
Wings ultra-sensitive
To solids   the ground not reflecting his breast
Feet tentatively out
Creaking   close   closer
Earth blurring   tilt back and brace
Against the wind   closest   touch

Sprawl.   In ridiculous wings, he flounders,
He waddles   he goes to sleep
In a stillness of body not otherwhere to be found
Upheld for one night
With his wings closed   the stiff land failing to rock him.

Here mating   the new life
Shall not be lost   wings tangle
Over the beaches   over the pale
Sketches of coral reefs   treading the air
The father moving almost
At once out the vast blue door
He feels it swing open
The island fall off him   the sun

Rise in the shape of an egg   enormous
Over the islands

250

                    passing out
Over the cliffs   scudding
Fifteen feet from the poor skinned sod
Dazing with purity the eyes of turtles
Lizards   then feeling the world at once
Sheerly restore the sea   the island not
Glanced back at   where the egg
Fills with almighty feathers
The dead rise, wrapped in their wings
The last thread of white
Is drawn from the foot of the cliffs
As the great sea takes itself back
From around the island

And he sails out   heads north
His eyes already on icebergs
Ten thousand miles off   already feeling
The shiver of the equator as it crosses
His body at its absolute
Midnight whiteness
                              and death also
Stands waiting   years away
In midair   beats
Balanced on starpoints
Latitude and longitude correct
Oriented by instinct   by stars
By the sun in one eye the moon
In the other   bird-death

Hovers for years on its wings
With a time sense that cannot fail
Waits to change
Him again   circles   abides   no feather
Falling   conceived by stars and the void
Is born perpetually
In midair   where it shall be
Where it is.

II

THE SHEEP CHILD

Farm boys wild to couple
With anything   with soft-wooded trees
With mounds of earth   mounds
Of pinestraw   will keep themselves off
Animals by legends of their own:
In the hay-tunnel dark
And dung of barns, they will
Say   I have heard tell

That in a museum in Atlanta
Way back in a corner somewhere
There's this thing that's only half
Sheep   like a woolly baby
Pickled in alcohol   because
Those things can't live.   his eyes
Are open   but you can't stand to look
I heard from somebody who . . .

But this is now almost all
Gone. The boys have taken
Their own true wives in the city,
The sheep are safe in the west hill
Pasture   but we who were born there
Still are not sure. Are we,
Because we remember, remembered
In the terrible dust of museums?

Merely with his eyes, the sheep-child may

Be saying   saying

> *I am here, in my father's house.*
> *I who am half of your world, came deeply*
> *To my mother in the long grass*

Of the west pasture, where she stood like moonlight
Listening for foxes. It was something like love
From another world that seized her
From behind, and she gave, not lifting her head
Out of dew, without ever looking, her best
Self to that great need. Turned loose, she dipped her face
Farther into the chill of the earth, and in a sound
Of sobbing   of something stumbling
Away, began, as she must do,
To carry me. I woke, dying,

In the summer sun of the hillside, with my eyes
Far more than human. I saw for a blazing moment
The great grassy world from both sides,
Man and beast in the round of their need,
And the hill wind stirred in my wool,
My hoof and my hand clasped each other,
I ate my one meal
Of milk, and died
Staring. From dark grass I came straight

To my father's house, whose dust
Whirls up in the halls for no reason
When no one comes   piling deep in a hellish mild corner,
And, through my immortal waters,
I meet the sun's grains eye
To eye, and they fail at my closet of glass.
Dead, I am most surely living
In the minds of farm boys: I am he who drives
Them like wolves from the hound bitch and calf
And from the chaste ewe in the wind.
They go into woods   into bean fields   they go
Deep into their known right hands. Dreaming of me,
They groan   they wait   they suffer
Themselves, they marry, they raise their kind.

SUN

O Lord, it was all night
Consuming me   skin crawling tighter than any
Skin of my teeth. Bleary with ointments, dazzling
Through the dark house   man red as iron   glowing
Blazing up anew with each bad
Breath from the bellowing curtains

I had held the sun longer
Than it could stay   and in the dark it turned
My face on, infra-red: there were cracks circling
My eyes where I had squinted
Up from stone-blind sand, and seen
Eternal fire   coronas   huge

Vertical banners of flame
Leap scrollingly from the sun and tatter
To nothing in blue-veined space
On the smoked-crimson glass of my lids.
When the sun fell, I slit my eyeskins
In the dazed ruddy muddle of twilight

And in the mirror saw whiteness
Run from my eyes like tears   going upward
And sideways   slanting   as well as falling,
All in straight lines like rays
Shining   and behind me, careful not
To touch without giving me a chance

To brace myself   a smeared
Suffering woman came merging her flame-shaken
Body halo with mine   her nose still clownish
With oxides: walked to me sweating
Blood, and turned around. I peeled off
Her bathing suit like her skin   her colors

Wincing   she silently biting
Her tongue off   her back crisscrossed with stripes
Where winter had caught her and whipped her.
We stumbled together, and in the double heat
The last of my blond hair blazed up,
Burned off me forever   as we dived

For the cool of the bed
In agony even at holding hands   the blisters
On our shoulders shifting   crackling
Releasing boiling water on the sheets. *O Lord*
Who can turn out the sun, turn out that neighbor's
One bulb on his badminton court

For we are dying
Of light   searing each other   not able
To stop   to get away   she screaming O Lord
Apollo or *Water, Water*   as the moonlight drove
Us down on the tangled grid
Where in the end we lay

Suffering equally   in the sun
Backlashed from the moon's brutal stone
And meeting itself where we had stored it up
All afternoon in pain   in the gentlest touch
As we lay, O Lord,
In Hell, in love.

POWER AND LIGHT

. . . only connect . . .
                —E. M. FORSTER

I may even be
A man, I tell my wife: all day I climb myself
Bowlegged up those damned poles   rooster-heeled in all
Kinds of weather   and what is there when I get
Home? Yes, woman trailing ground-oil
Like a snail, home is where I climb down,
And this is the house I pass through on my way

To power and light.
Going into the basement is slow, but the built-on smell of home
Beneath home gets better with age   the ground fermenting
And spilling through the barrel-cracks of plaster   the dark
Lying on the floor, ready for use   as I crack
The seal on the bottle   like I tell you it takes
A man to pour whiskey in the dark   and CLOSE THE DOOR between

The children and me.
The heads of nails drift deeper through their boards
And disappear. Years in the family dark have made me good
At this   nothing else is so good   pure fires of the Self
Rise crooning in lively blackness   and the silence around them,
Like the silence inside a mouth, squirms with colors,
The marvellous worms of the eye float out into the real

World   sunspots
Dancing as though existence were
One huge closed eye   and I feel the wires running
Like the life-force along the limed rafters   and all connections
With poles   with the tarred naked belly-buckled black
Trees I hook to my heels   with the shrill phone calls leaping
Long distance   long distances through my hands   all connections

Even the one
With my wife, turn good   turn better than good   turn good
Not quite, but in the deep sway of underground   among the roots

That bend like branches   all things connect   and stream
Toward light and speech   tingle   rock like a powerline in wind,
Like a man working, drunk on pine-moves   the sun in the socket
Of his shoulder   and on his neck dancing like dice-dots,

And I laugh
Like my own fate watching over me night and day   at home
Underground   or flung up on towers walking
Over mountains   my charged hair standing on end   crossing
The sickled, slaughtered alleys of timber
Where the lines loop and crackle on their gallows.
Far under the grass of my grave, I drink like a man

The night before
Resurrection Day. My watch glows with the time to rise
And shine. Never think I don't know my profession
Will lift me: why, all over hell the lights burn in your eyes,
People are calling each other   weeping with a hundred thousand
Volts   making deals   pleading   laughing like fate,
Far off, invulnerable   or with the right word pierced

To the heart
By wires I held, shooting off their ghostly mouths,
In my gloves. The house spins   I strap crampons to my shoes
To climb the basement stairs, sinking my heels in the tree-
life of the boards. Thorns! Thorns! I am bursting
Into the kitchen, into the sad way-station
Of my home, holding a double handful of wires

Spitting like sparklers
On the Fourth of July. Woman, I know the secret of sitting
In light   of eating a limp piece of bread   under
The red-veined eyeball of a bulb. It is all in how you are
Grounded. To bread I can see, I say, as it disappears and agrees
With me   the dark is drunk   and I am a man
Who turns on. I am a man.

THE FLASH

Something far off   buried deep and free
In the country   can always strike you dead
Center of the brain. There is never anything

It could be   but you go dazzled
Dazzled   and all the air in that
Direction swarms   waits

For that day-lightning,
For hoe blade   buckle   bifocal
To reach you. Whatever it does

Again is worth waiting for
Worth stopping the car   worth standing alone
For   and arranging the body

For light to score off you
In its own way, and send
Across the wheat   the broad silent

Blue valley, your long-awaited,
Blinding, blood-brotherly
Beyond-speech answer.

ADULTERY

We have all been in rooms
We cannot die in, and they are odd places, and sad.
Often Indians are standing eagle-armed on hills

In the sunrise   open wide to the Great Spirit
Or gliding in canoes   or cattle are browsing on the walls
Far away   gazing down with the eyes of our children

Not far away   or there are men driving
The last railspike, which has turned
Gold in their hands. Gigantic forepleasure lives

Among such scenes, and we are alone with it
At last. There is always some weeping
Between us   and someone is always checking

A wrist watch by the bed to see how much
Longer we have left. Nothing can come
Of this   nothing can come

Of us: of me with my grim techniques
Or you who have sealed your womb
With a ring of convulsive rubber:

Although we come together,
Nothing will come of us. But we would not give
It up, for death is beaten

By praying Indians   by distant cows   historical
Hammers   by hazardous meetings that bridge
A continent. One could never die here

Never die   never die
While crying. My lover, my dear one
I will see you next week

When I'm in town. I will call you
If I can. Please get hold of   please don't
Oh God, Please don't any more I can't bear . . . Listen:

We have done it again   we are
Still living. Sit up and smile,
God bless you. Guilt is magical.

HEDGE LIFE

At morning we all look out
As our dwelling lightens; we have been somewhere.
With dew our porous home
Is dense, wound up like a spring,

Which is solid as motherlode
At night. Those who live in these apartments
Exist for the feeling of growth
As thick as it can get, but filled with

Concealment. When lightning
Strikes us, we are safe; there is nothing to strike, no bole
For all-fire's shattered right arm.
We are small creatures, surviving

On the one breath that grows
In our lungs in the complex green, reassured in the dawn-
silver heavy as wool. We wait
With crowded excitement

For our house to spring
Slowly out of night-wet to the sun; beneath us,
The moon hacked to pieces on the ground.
None but we are curled

Here, rising another inch,
Knowing that what held us solid in the moon is still
With us, where the outside flowers flash
In bits, creatures travel

Beyond us like rain,
The great sun floats in a fringed bag, all stones quiver
With the wind that moves us.
We trade laughters silently

Back and forth, and feel,
As we dreamed we did last night, our noses safe in our fur,
That what is happening to us in our dwelling
Is true: That on either side

As we sleep, as we wake, as we rise
Like springs, the house is winding away across the fields,
Stopped only momentarily by roads,
King-walking hill after hill.

SNAKEBITE

I am the one

And there is no way not
To be me   not to have been flagged

Down from underneath where back
Drop ten deadly and
Dead pine logs   here and where
They have fallen. Now come

To surprise:

Surprise at the dosage   at the shot
In the foot   at the ground

Where I walk   at what
It can do and the ways
Of giving: at dry fish scales
That can float away

In a long dusty arm

Now getting itself   frankly lost
Swimming against the current

Of pinestraw   winging under a stump
And a stone. Here is where
I am the one chosen:
Something has licked my heel

Like a surgeon

And I have a problem with
My right foot and my life.

It is hard to think of dying
But not of killing: hold the good
Foot ready to put on his head
Except that it leaves me only

On a stage of pine logs

Something like an actor   so
Let me sit down and draw

My tiny sword   unfold it
Where the dead sharpen needles
By the million. It is the role
I have been cast in;

It calls for blood.

Act it out before the wind
Blows: unspilt blood

Will kill you. Open
The new-footed tingling. Cut.
Cut deep, as a brother would.
Cut to save it. Me.

BREAD

Old boys, the cracked boards spread before
You, bread and spam   fruit cocktail   powder
Of eggs. I who had not risen, but just come down
From the night sky   knew always this was nothing
Like home   for under the table I was cut deep
  In the shoes

To make them like sandals no stateside store
Ever sold   and my shirtsleeves were ragged as
Though chopped off by propellers in the dark.
It was all our squadron, old boys: it was thus
I sat with you on your first morning
  On the earth,

Old boys newly risen from a B-25 sinking slowly
Into the swamps of Ceram. Patrick said
We got out   we got out on the wings
And lived there   we spread our weight
Thin as we could   arms and legs spread, we lay
  Down night and day,

We lived on the wings. When one of us got to one
Knee to spear a frog   to catch a snake
To eat, we lost another inch. O that water,
He said. O that water. Old boys, when you first
Rose, I sat with you in the mess-tent
  On solid ground,

At the unsinkable feast, and looked at the bread
Given to lizard-eaters. They set it down
And it glowed from under   your tongues
Fluttered   you reached   the scales fell
From your eyes   all of us weightless from living
  On wings so long

No one could escape   no one could sink or swim
Or fly. I looked at your yellow eyeballs
Come up   evolved   drawn out of the world's slime

Amphibious eyes   and Patrick said Bread
Is good   I sat with you in my own last war
     Poem   I closed my eyes

I ate the food I ne'er had eat.

SUSTAINMENT

Here at the level of leaves supposedly for good
Stopped dead on the ground,
From the safety of picturesque height she was suddenly
Falling into the creek, the path
That held her become a flight of dirt. She
And the horse screamed all together, and went down.

Not knowing her, but knowing who she was
Before the creek bank gave
Way and the hooves broke through into creek-shaped air,
I come walking past all the remaining leaves
At the edge, knowing the snow of dirt
Down the bank has long since stopped,

Seeing the gap in the ledge above the stream
Still hold the print
Of a horse's head-down side, aware that I can stoop
With my love, who is with me, and feel
The earth of that blurred impression
Where it is cold with time and many unmeaningful rains.

Love, this wood can support our passion, though leaves
Are not enough death
To balance what we must act out. Let me double down
My autumn raincoat near the summer pit
Where the unknowable woman was riding proudly
The high crest of June, her pink shirt open-throated,

Her four hooves knocking deeply on the earth, the water
Unconsciously holding
Its flow in the pressure of sunlight, a snail
Glinting like a molar at the brink,
And felt it all give way in one clear scream
Lifted out the horse through her lipsticked mouth,

And then, ripping the path clean out of the woods,
Landslid down fifty feet,
Snapping high-grade leather, past any help in the world

As the horse turned over her, in a long changed shape
Loomed once, crossed the sun and the upper trees
Like a myth with a hold on her feet, and fell on her

With all his intended mass. Know, love, that we
Shall rise from here
Where she did not, lying now where we have come
Beneath the scrambling animal weight
Of lust, but that we may sense also
What it involves to change in one half-breath

From a thing half-beast—that huge-striding joy
Between the thighs—
To the wholly human in time
To die, here at this height
Near the vague body-print of a being that struggled
Up, all animal, leaving the human clothes

In their sodden bundle, and wandered the lane of water
Upstream and home,
His bridle dragging, his saddle
Maniacally wrenched, stopping often to drink
Entirely, his eyes receiving bright pebbles,
His head in his own image where it flowed.

A LETTER

Looking out of the dark of the town
At midnight, looking down
Into water under the lighthouse:
Abstractedly, timelessly looking
For something beneath the jetty,
Waiting for the dazed, silent flash,

Like the painless explosion that kills one,
To come from above and slide over
And empty the surface for miles—
The useless, imperial sweep
Of utter light—you see
A thicket of little fish

Below the squared stone of your window,
Catching, as it passes,
The blue afterthought of the blaze.
Shone almost into full being,
Inlaid in frail gold in their floor,
Their collected vision sways

Like dust among them;
You can see the essential spark
Of sight, of intuition,
Travel from eye to eye.
The next leg of light that comes round
Shows nothing where they have been,

But words light up in the head
To take their deep place in the darkness,
Arcing quickly from image to image
Like mica catching the sun:
The words of a love letter,
Of a letter to a long-dead father,

To an unborn son, to a woman
Long another man's wife, to her children,
To anyone out of reach, not born,

Or dead, who lives again,
Is born, is young, is the same:
Anyone who can wait no longer

Beneath the huge blackness of time
Which lies concealing, concealing
What must gleam forth in the end,
Glimpsed, unchanging, and gone
When memory stands without sleep
And gets its strange spark from the world.

THE HEAD-AIM

Sick of your arms,
You must follow an endless track

Into the world that crawls,
That gets up on four legs
When the moon rises from a bed of grass,
The night one vast and vivid
Tangle of scents.

You must throw your arms
Like broken sticks into the alder creek

And learn to aim the head.
There is nothing you can pick up
With fingers any more, nothing
But the new head choked with long teeth,
The jaws, on fire with rabies,

Lifting out of the weeds.
This is the whole secret of being

Inhuman: to aim the head as you should,
And to hold back in the body
What the mouth might otherwise speak:
Immortal poems—those matters of life and death—
When the lips curl back

And the eyes prepare to sink
Also, in the jerking fur of the other.

Fox, marten, weasel,
No one can give you hands.
Let the eyes see death say it all
Straight into your oncoming face, the head
Not fail, not tell.

DARK ONES

We in all lights are coming
Home   transfixed and carried away
From where we work:
                    when the sun moves down
The railroad tracks, and dies a little way
Off in the weeds, lights we have made come on
And carry us: this is how
We are coming, O all
Our dark ones, our darlings.

Now we float down from aircraft

From trains   now at our car
Lights the doors
                    of our home
Garage spring open   we enter and fall
Down in our souls to pray for light
To fail: fail pleasantly with gin,
With problems of children   but fail   fade
Back into our tinted walls:

Let the airports carry it all night

Let the highways support it on their poles
Shining on beer cans
                    rolling drunk in the weeds
After their one fearful bounce:
Lord, let those lights give up
On us: office lights, cast like shade
On fire, from their banks of blue sticks:
A light like the mange, on papers,

On the heads emerging from scratch pads,

Those crammed, volcanic faces
Dreadful to see.
                    All those are creatures
Of light. Let them leave me   let all

Human switches be finally snapped
Off at once   let me go with my dark
Darling, into myself: O let there be
Someone in it with me:

Let us move everything

Off us, and lie touching
With all we have.
                              O creature
Of darkness, let us lie stretched out
Without shadow or weight.
Fasten your hand where my heart
Would burst, if I moved
From your side. You are

Who holds. Hold then   hold my heart

Down from bursting
Into light: hold it still and at rest
In the center of walls
That cannot get their colors
Back without light: O Glory, there is nothing
Yet at the sill   no grain or thread
Of sun   no light as the heart

Beats, feeding from your hand.

ENCOUNTER IN THE CAGE COUNTRY

What I was would not work
For them all, for I had not caught
The lion's eye. I was walking down

The cellblock in green glasses   and came
At last to the place where someone was hiding
His spots in his black hide.

Unchangeably they were there,
Driven in as by eyes
Like mine, his darkness ablaze

In the stinking sun of the beast house.
Among the crowd, he found me
Out   and dropped his bloody snack

And came to the perilous edge
Of the cage, where the great bars tremble
Like wire. All Sunday ambling stopped,

The curved cells tightened around
Us all   as we saw he was watching only
Me. I knew the stage was set, and I began

To perform   first saunt'ring   then stalking
Back and forth like a sentry   faked
As if to run   and at one brilliant move

I made as though drawing a gun from my hip-
bone, the bite-sized children broke
Up   changing their concept of laughter,

But none of this changed his eyes, or changed
My green glasses. Alert, attentive,
He waited for what I could give him:

My moves   my throat   my wildest love,
The eyes behind my eyes. Instead, I left
Him, though he followed me right to the end

Of concrete. I wiped my face, and lifted off
My glasses. Light blasted the world of shade
Back under every park bush   the crowd

Quailed from me   I was inside and out
Of myself   and something was given a life-
mission to say to me hungrily over

And over and over   *your moves are exactly right*
For a few things in this world: we know you
When you come, Green Eyes, Green Eyes.

FOR THE LAST WOLVERINE

They will soon be down

To one, but he still will be
For a little while   still will be stopping

The flakes in the air with a look,
Surrounding himself with the silence
Of whitening snarls. Let him eat
The last red meal of the condemned

To extinction, tearing the guts

From an elk. Yet that is not enough
For me. I would have him eat

The heart, and, from it, have an idea
Stream into his gnawing head
That he no longer has a thing
To lose, and so can walk

Out into the open, in the full

Pale of the sub-Arctic sun
Where a single spruce tree is dying

Higher and higher. Let him climb it
With all his meanness and strength.
Lord, we have come to the end
Of this kind of vision of heaven,

As the sky breaks open

Its fans around him and shimmers
And into its northern gates he rises

Snarling   complete   in the joy of a weasel
With an elk's horned heart in his stomach
Looking straight into the eternal

Blue, where he hauls his kind. I would have it all

My way: at the top of that tree I place

The New World's last eagle
Hunched in mangy feathers   giving

Up on the theory of flight.
Dear God of the wildness of poetry, let them mate
To the death in the rotten branches,
Let the tree sway and burst into flame

And mingle them, crackling with feathers,

In crownfire. Let something come
Of it   something gigantic   legendary

Rise beyond reason over hills
Of ice   SCREAMING   that it cannot die,
That it has come back, this time
On wings, and will spare no earthly thing:

That it will hover, made purely of northern

Lights, at dusk   and fall
On men building roads: will perch

On the moose's horn like a falcon
Riding into battle   into holy war against
Screaming railroad crews: will pull
Whole traplines like fibres from the snow

In the long-jawed night of fur trappers.

But, small, filthy, unwinged,
You will soon be crouching

Alone, with maybe some dim racial notion
Of being the last, but none of how much
Your unnoticed going will mean:

How much the timid poem needs

The mindless explosion of your rage,

The glutton's internal fire   the elk's
Heart in the belly, sprouting wings,

The pact of the "blind swallowing
Thing," with himself, to eat
The world, and not to be driven off it
Until it is gone, even if it takes

Forever. I take you as you are

And make of you what I will,
Skunk-bear, carcajou, bloodthirsty

Non-survivor.
                Lord, let me die   but not die
Out.

THE BEE

To the football coaches of Clemson College, 1942

One dot
Grainily shifting   we at roadside and
The smallest wings coming   along the rail fence out
Of the woods   one dot   of all that green. It now
Becomes flesh-crawling   then the quite still
Of stinging. I must live faster for my terrified
Small son   it is on him. Has come. Clings.

Old wingback, come
To life. If your knee action is high
Enough, the fat may fall in time   God damn
You, Dickey, *dig*   this is your last time to cut
And run   but you must give it everything you have
Left, for screaming near your screaming child is the sheer
Murder of California traffic: some bee hangs driving

Your child
Blindly onto the highway. Get there however
Is still possible. Long live what I badly did
At Clemson   and all of my clumsiest drives
For the ball   all of my trying to turn
The corner downfield   and my spindling explosions
Through the five-hole over tackle. O backfield

Coach Shag Norton,
Tell me as you never yet have told me
To get the lead out   scream whatever will get
The slow-motion of middle age off me   I cannot
Make it this way   I will have to leave
My feet   they are gone   I have him where
He lives   and down we go singing with screams into

The dirt,
Son-screams of fathers   screams of dead coaches turning
To approval   and from between us the bee rises screaming

With flight   grainily shifting   riding the rail fence
Back into the woods   traffic blasting past us
Unchanged, nothing heard through the air-
conditioning glass   we lying at roadside full

Of the forearm prints
Of roadrocks   strawberries on our elbows as from
Scrimmage with the varsity   now we can get
Up   stand   turn away from the highway   look straight
Into trees. See, there is nothing coming out   no
Smallest wing   no shift of a flight-grain   nothing
Nothing. Let us go in, son, and listen

For some tobacco-
mumbling voice in the branches   to say "That's
a little better,"   to our lives still hanging
By a hair. There is nothing to stop us   we can go
Deep   deeper   into elms, and listen to traffic die
Roaring, like a football crowd from which we have
Vanished. Dead coaches live in the air, son   live

In the ear
Like fathers, and *urge*   and *urge*. They want you better
Than you are. When needed, they rise and curse you   they scream
When something must be saved. Here, under this tree,
We can sit down. You can sleep, and I can try
To give back what I have earned by keeping us
Alive, and safe from bees: the smile of some kind

Of savior—
Of touchdowns, of fumbles, battles,
Lives. Let me sit here with you, son
As on the bench, while the first string takes back
Over, far away   and say with my silentest tongue, with the man-
creating bruises of my arms   with a live leaf a quick
Dead hand on my shoulder, "Coach Norton, I am your boy."

MARY SHEFFIELD

Forever at war news   I am
thinking there   nearly naked
low green of water   hard overflowed forms

water sits running   quietly carving
red rocks forcing white from the current

parts of midstream   join
I sit with one hand   joining
the other hand shyly   fine sand under

still feet   and Mary Sheffield
singing   passed-through

sustained in the   poured forms of live oaks
taking root   in the last tracks
of left and right foot   river flowing

into my mind   nearly naked
the last day but one   before world war.

When the slight wind dies
each leaf still has   two places
such music   touched alive

guitar strings   sounds   join
In the stone's shoal   of swimming

the best twigs I have   the best
sailing leaves   in memory
pass   threading through

all things spread sail   sounds gather
on blunt stone   streaming white

E minor   gently running
I sit with one hand   in the strange life
of the other   watching water throng

on one stone   loving Mary Sheffield
for her chord changes   river always

before war   I sit down and
anywhere   water flows   the breastplate of time
rusts off me   sounds   green forms   low voice

new music   long   long
past.

DEER AMONG CATTLE

Here and there in the searing beam
Of my hand going through the night meadow
They all are grazing

With pins of human light in their eyes.
A wild one also is eating
The human grass,

Slender, graceful, domesticated
By darkness, among the bred-
for-slaughter,

Having bounded their paralyzed fence
And inclined his branched forehead onto
Their green frosted table,

The only live thing in this flashlight
Who can leave whenever he wishes,
Turn grass into forest,

Foreclose inhuman brightness from his eyes
But stands here still, unperturbed,
In their wide-open country,

The sparks from my hand in his pupils
Unmatched anywhere among cattle,

Grazing with them the night of the hammer
As one of their own who shall rise.

THE LEAP

The only thing I have of Jane MacNaughton
Is one instant of a dancing-class dance.
She was the fastest runner in the seventh grade,
My scrapbook says, even when boys were beginning
To be as big as the girls,
But I do not have her running in my mind,
Though Frances Lane is there, Agnes Fraser,
Fat Betty Lou Black in the boys-against-girls
Relays we ran at recess: she must have run

Like the other girls, with her skirts tucked up
So they would be like bloomers,
But I cannot tell; that part of her is gone.
What I do have is when she came,
With the hem of her skirt where it should be
For a young lady, into the annual dance
Of the dancing class we all hated, and with a light
Grave leap, jumped up and touched the end
Of one of the paper-ring decorations

To see if she could reach it. She could,
And reached me now as well, hanging in my mind
From a brown chain of brittle paper, thin
And muscular, wide-mouthed, eager to prove
Whatever it proves when you leap
In a new dress, a new womanhood, among the boys
Whom you easily left in the dust
Of the passionless playground. If I said I saw
In the paper where Jane MacNaughton Hill,

Mother of four, leapt to her death from a window
Of a downtown hotel, and that her body crushed-in
The top of a parked taxi, and that I held
Without trembling a picture of her lying cradled
In that papery steel as though lying in the grass,
One shoe idly off, arms folded across her breast,
I would not believe myself. I would say
The convenient thing, that it was a bad dream

Of maturity, to see that eternal process

Most obsessively wrong with the world
Come out of her light, earth-spurning feet
Grown heavy: would say that in the dusty heels
Of the playground some boy who did not depend
On speed of foot, caught and betrayed her.
Jane, stay where you are in my first mind:
It was odd in that school, at that dance.
I and the other slow-footed yokels sat in corners
Cutting rings out of drawing paper

Before you leapt in your new dress
And touched the end of something I began,
Above the couples struggling on the floor,
New men and women clutching at each other
And prancing foolishly as bears: hold on
To that ring I made for you, Jane—
My feet are nailed to the ground
By dust I swallowed thirty years ago—
While I examine my hands.

COMING BACK TO AMERICA

We descended the first night from Europe   riding the ship's sling
Into the basement.   Forty floors of home weighed on us.   We broke
    through
To a room, and fell to drinking madly with all those boozing, reading
The Gideon Bible in a dazzle of homecoming scripture   Assyrian
    armies
The scythes of chariots blazing like the windows of the city   all cast
Into our eyes in all-night squinting barbaric rays of violent unavoidable
    glory.
There were a "million dollars in ice cubes" outside our metal door;
The dead water clattered down hour after hour as we fought with
    salesmen
For the little blocks that would make whole our long savage drinks.
I took a swaying shower, and we packed the whole bathroom of towels
    into
Our dusty luggage, battling paid-for opulence with whatever weapon
Came to hand.   We slept; I woke up early, knowing that I was
    suffering
But why not. My breath would not stir, nor the room's.   I sweated
Ice in the closeness   my head hurt with the Sleep of a Thousand Lights
That the green baize drapes could not darken.   I got up, bearing
Everything   found my sharp Roman shoes   went out   following
    signs
That said Swimming Pool.   Flashing bulbs on a red-eyed panel,
    I passed
Through ceiling after ceiling of sleeping salesmen and whores, and
    came out
On the roof.   The pool water trembled with the few in their rooms
Still making love.   This was air.   A skinny girl lifeguard worked
At her nails; the dawn shone on her right leg in a healthy, twisted flame.
It made me squint   slick and lacquered with scars   with the wild
    smoky city
Around it   the great breath to be drawn above sleepers   the hazy
Morning towers.   We sat and talked   she said a five-car wreck
Of taxis in Bensonhurst had knocked her out and taken her kneecap
But nothing else.   I pondered this   the sun shook off a last heavy
Hotel   and she leapt and was in the fragile green pool as though
I were still sleeping it off eleven floors under her: she turned in a water

Ballet by herself   graceful   unredeemable   her tough face exactly
As beautiful and integral as the sun come out of the city.   Vulnerable,
Hurt in my country's murderous speed, she moved   and I would have
    taken
Her in my arms in water throbbing with the passion of travelling men,
Unkillable, both of us, at forty stories in the morning   and could have
Flown with her   our weightlessness preserved by the magic pool
    drawn from
Under the streets   out of that pond   passing over the meaningless
Guardrail   feeling the whole air pulse like water sleepless with
    desperate
Love-making   lifting us out of sleep into the city summer dawn
Of hundreds of feet of gray space spinning with pigeons now under
Us   among new panels of sun in the buildings blasting light silently
Back and forth across streets between them: could have moved with her
In all this   over the floods of glare raised up in sheets   the gauze
Distances where warehouses strove to become   over the ship I had
    ridden
Home in   riding gently   whitely   beneath.   Ah, lift us, green
City water, as we turn the harbor around with our legs   lazily changing
The plan of the city with motions like thistles   like the majestic swirl
Of soot   the winged seed of pigeons   and so would have held her
As I held my head   a-stammer with light   defending it against the
    terrible
Morning sun of drinkers   in that pain, exhalting in the blind notion
Of cradling her somewhere above ships and buses   in the air like a
    water
Ballet   dancing deep among the dawn buildings in a purely private
Embrace of impossibility   a love that could not have been guessed:
Woman   being   idea   temple dancer   tough girl from Bensonhurst
With a knee rebuilt out of sunlight   returned-to amazement
    O claspable
Symbol   the unforeseen on home ground   The thing that sustains
    us forever
In other places!

III

THE BIRTHDAY DREAM

At the worst place in the hills above the city
Late at night I was driving   cutting through
The overbalancing slums. There was no soul or body
In the streets. I turned right   then left somewhere
Near the top, dead-ending into a wall. A car
Pulled out and blocked me. Four men detached from it.
I got out too. It was Saturday night   the thrill
Of trouble shimmered on the concrete. One shadow
Had a bottle of wine. I stood and said, say, Buddy,
Give me a drink of that wine   not at all fearing
Shaking   as on anything but dream bones   dream
Feet I would have. He said, We're looking for somebody
To beat up. It won't be me, I said   and took him
By the arm with one hand and tossed him into the air.
Snow fell from the clearness in time for there
To be a snowbank for him to fall into elbow-first.
He got up, holding the wine. This guy is too big,
He said, he is too big for us; get the Professor.
Four of us stood together as the wind blew and the snow
Disappeared   and watched the lights of the city
Shine   some others appearing   among them   some
Going out   and watched the lava-flow of headlights off
In the valley. Like a gunshot in the building next to us
A light went out   and down came a middle-aged man
With a hairy chest; his gold-trimmed track shorts had
YMCA Instructor on them   and I knew it was time
For the arm game. We stretched out on our stomachs
On top of the dead-end wall. On one side was the drop
We had all been looking into   and the other side sank
Away with my car   with the men: two darks lifted
Us toward the moon. We put our elbows on the wall
And clasped palms. Something had placed gold-rimmed
Glasses of wine beside us   apartment lights hung in them
Loosely   and we lay nose to nose at the beginning

288

Of that ceremony; I saw the distant traffic cross him
From eye to eye. Slowly I started to push   and he
To push. My body grew as it lay   forced against his
But nothing moved. I could feel the blood vessels
In my brow distend   extend   grow over the wall like vines
And in my neck   swell like a trumpet player's: I gritted
Into his impassive face   where the far lights moved   this is
What I want   this is what I came for. The city pulsed
And trembled in my arm   shook with my effort   for miles
In every direction   and from far below in the dark
I heard the voices of men raised up in a cry of wild
Encouragement   of terror   joy   as I strained to push
His locked hand down. I could not move him   did not want
To move him   would not yield. The world strove with my body
To overcome   the highways shuddered   writhed   came apart
At the centerline   far below us a silent train went by
A warning light   and slowly from the embodying air was loaded
With thousands of ghostly new cars   in tiered racks
The light like pale wine in their tinted windshields.
The culture swarmed around me like my blood   transfigured
By force. I put my head down and pushed with all my life
And writing sprang under my forehead   onto the concrete:
Graffitti scratched with a nail   a boot heel   an ice pick
A tire iron   a scrap of metal from a stolen car   saying
You are here   and I woke
Entangled with my wife, who labored   pled   screamed
To bring me forth. The room was full of mildness. I was forty.

FALSE YOUTH: TWO SEASONS

I

I have had my time   dressed up as something else,
Have thrown time off my track by my disguise.
This can happen when one puts on a hunter's cap,
An unearned cowboy hat   a buckskin coat   or something
From outer space, that a child you have got has got
For Christmas. It is oddest and best in the uniform
Of your country   long laid in boxes and now let out
To hold the self-betrayed form in the intolerant shape
Of its youth.   I have had my time doing such,

Sitting with Phyllis Huntley as though I were my own
Son surrounded by wisteria   hearing mosquitoes without
The irritation middle age puts on their wings: have sat
By a big vine going round the rotten, imperial pillars
Of southern Mississippi. All family sounds drew back

Through the house in time to leave us hanging
By rusty chains. In the dark, dressed up in my militant youth,
I might have just come down from the black sky   alive
With an ancient war   dead with twenty million   twenty
Years ago   when my belt cried aloud for more holes
And I soft-saluted every changing shape   that saluted me,
And many that did not: every tree   pole   every bush
Of wisteria   as I came down from the air toward some girl

Or other. Decked out in something strange my country
Dreamed up   I have had my time in that swing,
The double chair that moves at the edge of dark
Where the years stand just out of range of house-
light, their hands folded at their fat waists, respectful
As figures at a funeral. And from out of the air an enormous
Grin came down, to remake my face   as I thought of children
Of mine almost her age   and a mosquito droned like an immortal
Engine. I have had my time of moving back and forth
With Phyllis Huntley   and of the movement of her small hand
Inside mine, as she told me how she learned to work
An electric computer in less than two afternoons of her job

At the air base. The uniform tightened as I sat
Debating with a family man away from home. I would not listen
To him, for what these boys want is to taste a little life
Before they die: that is when their wings begin to shine
Most brilliantly from their breasts into the darkness
And the beery breath of a fierce boy demands of the fat man
He's dying of   more air   more air   through the tight belt
Of time   more life   more now   than when death was faced
Less slowly   more now than then   more now.

      II

Through an ice storm in Nashville I took a student home,
Sliding off the road twice or three times; for this
She asked me in. She was a living-in-the-city
Country girl   who on her glazed porch broke off
An icicle, and bit through its blank bone: brought me
Into another life   in the shining-skinned clapboard house
Surrounded by a world where creatures could not stand,
Where people broke hip after hip. At the door my feet
Took hold, and at the fire I sat down with her blind
Grandmother. All over the double room were things
That would never freeze, but would have taken well
To ice: long tassels hanging from lamps   curtains
Of beads   a shawl on the mantel   all endless things
To touch   untangle   all things intended to be
Inexhaustible to hands. She sat there, fondling
What was in reach   staring into the fire with me
Never batting a lid. I talked to her easily   eagerly
Of my childhood   my mother whistling in her heartsick bed
My father grooming his gamecocks. She rocked, fingering
The lace on the arm of the chair   changing its pattern
Like a game of chess. Before I left, she turned and raised
Her hands, and asked me to bend down. An icicle stiffened
In my stomach   as she drew on my one lock of hair
Feeling the individual rare strands   not pulling any
Out. I closed my eyes as she put her fingertips lightly
On them   and saw, behind sight   something in me   fire
Swirl in a great shape like a fingerprint   like none other
In the history of the earth   looping   holding its wild lines
Of human force. Her forefinger   then her keen nail

Went all the way along the deep middle line of my brow
Not guessing but knowing   quivering   deepening
Whatever I showed by it. She said, you must laugh a lot
Or be in the sun, and I began to laugh quietly against
The truth, so she might feel what the line she followed
Did then. Her hands fell   and she said to herself, My God,
To have a growing boy. You cannot fool the blind, I knew
As I battled for air   standing   laughing a lot as she
Said I must do   squinting also as in the brightest sun
In Georgia   to make good   to make good the line in my head.
She lifted her face like a swimmer; the fire swarmed
On my false, created visage   as she rocked and took up
The tassel of a lamp. Some kind of song may have passed
Between our closed mouths as I headed   into the ice.
My face froze with the vast world of time   in a smile
That has never left me since my thirty-eighth year
When I skated like an out-of-shape bear to my Chevrolet
And spun my wheels on glass: that time when age was caught
In a thaw in a ravelling room   when I conceived of my finger
Print as a shape of fire   and of youth as a lifetime search
For the blind.

FALLING

*A 29-year-old stewardess fell . . . to her
death tonight when she was swept
through an emergency door that suddenly sprang open . . . The body . . .
was found . . . three hours after the
accident.*
　　　　　　　　　—New York Times

The states when they black out and lie there rolling　　when they turn
To something transcontinental　　move by　　drawing moonlight out
　　of the great
One-sided stone hung off the starboard wingtip　　some sleeper next to
An engine is groaning for coffee　　and there is faintly coming in
Somewhere the vast beast-whistle of space. In the galley with its racks
Of trays　　she rummages for a blanket　　and moves in her slim tailored
Uniform to pin it over the cry at the top of the door. As though she blew

The door down with a silent blast from her lungs　　frozen　　she is black
Out finding herself　　with the plane nowhere and her body taking by
　　the throat
The undying cry of the void　　falling　　living　　beginning to be
　　something
That no one has ever been and lived through　　screaming without
　　enough air
Still neat　　lipsticked　　stockinged　　girdled by regulation　　her hat
Still on　　her arms and legs in no world　　and yet spaced also strangely
With utter placid rightness on thin air　　taking her time　　she holds it
In many places　　and now, still thousands of feet from her death
　　she seems
To slow　　she develops interest　　she turns in her maneuverable body

To watch it. She is hung high up in the overwhelming middle of things
　　in her
Self　　in low body-whistling wrapped intensely　　in all her dark
　　dance-weight
Coming down from a marvellous leap　　with the delaying,
　　dumfounding ease
Of a dream of being drawn　　like endless moonlight to the harvest soil
Of a central state of one's country　　with a great gradual warmth

Falling　293

coming
Over her   floating   finding more and more breath in what she has
    been using
For breath   as the levels become more human   seeing clouds placed
    honestly
Below her left and right   riding slowly toward them   she clasps it all
To her and can hang her hands and feet in it in peculiar ways   and
Her eyes opened wide by wind, can open her mouth as wide   wider
    and suck
All the heat from the cornfields   can go down on her back with a
    feeling
Of stupendous pillows stacked under her   and can turn   turn as
    to someone
In bed   smile, understood in darkness   can go away   slant   slide
Off tumbling   into the emblem of a bird with its wings half-spread
Or whirl madly on herself   in endless gymnastics in the growing
    warmth
Of wheatfields rising toward the harvest moon.   There is time to live
In superhuman health   seeing mortal unreachable lights far down
    seeing
An ultimate highway with one late priceless car probing it   arriving
In a square town   and off her starboard arm the glitter of water catches
The moon by its one shaken side   scaled, roaming silver   My God
    it is good
And evil   lying in one after another of all the positions for love
Making   dancing   sleeping   and now cloud wisps at her no
Raincoat   no matter   all small towns brokenly brighter from inside
Cloud   she walks over them like rain   bursts out to behold a
    Greyhound
Bus shooting light through its sides   it is the signal to go straight
Down like a glorious diver   then feet first   her skirt stripped
    beautifully
Up   her face in fear-scented cloths   her legs deliriously bare   then
Arms out   she slow-rolls over   steadies out   waits for something
    great
To take control of her   trembles near feathers   planes head-down
The quick movements of bird-necks turning her head   gold eyes
    the insight-
eyesight of owls blazing into the hencoops   a taste for chicken
    overwhelming

294

Her   the long-range vision of hawks enlarging all human lights
     of cars
Freight trains   looped bridges   enlarging the moon racing slowly
Through all the curves of a river   all the darks of the midwest blazing
From above. A rabbit in a bush turns white   the smothering chickens
Huddle   for over them there is still time for something to live
With the streaming half-idea of a long stoop   a hurtling   a fall
That is controlled   that plummets as it wills   turns gravity
Into a new condition, showing its other side like a moon   shining
New Powers   there is still time to live on a breath made of nothing
But the whole night   time for her to remember to arrange her skirt
Like a diagram of a bat   tightly it guides her   she has this flying-skin
Made of garments   and there are also those sky-divers on TV   sailing
In sunlight   smiling under their goggles   swapping batons back
     and forth
And He who jumped without a chute and was handed one by a diving
Buddy. She looks for her grinning companion   white teeth   nowhere
She is screaming   singing hymns   her thin human wings spread out
From her neat shoulders   the air beast-crooning to her   warbling
And she can no longer behold the huge partial form of the world   now
She is watching her country lose its evoked master shape   watching
     it lose
And gain   get back its houses and peoples   watching it bring up
Its local lights   single homes   lamps on barn roofs   if she fell
Into water she might live   like a diver   cleaving   perfect   plunge

Into another   heavy silver   unbreathable   slowing   saving
Element: there is water   there is time to perfect all the fine
Points of diving   feet together   toes pointed   hands shaped right
To insert her into water like a needle   to come out healthily dripping
And be handed a Coca-Cola   there they are   there are the waters
Of life   the moon packed and coiled in a reservoir   so let me begin
To plane across the night air of Kansas   opening my eyes
     superhumanly
Bright   to the dammed moon   opening the natural wings of my jacket
By Don Loper   moving like a hunting owl toward the glitter of water
One cannot just fall   just tumble screaming all that time   one must use
It   she is now through with all   through all   clouds   damp   hair
Straightened   the last wisp of fog pulled apart on her face like wool
     revealing

New darks   new progressions of headlights along dirt roads
     from chaos

And night   a gradual warming   a new-made, inevitable world of
     one's own
Country   a great stone of light in its waiting waters   hold   hold out
For water: who knows when what correct young woman must take up
     her body
And fly   and head for the moon-crazed inner eye of midwest
     imprisoned
Water   stored up for her for years   the arms of her jacket slipping
Air up her sleeves to go   all over her? What final things can be said
Of one who starts out sheerly in her body in the high middle of night
Air   to track down water like a rabbit where it lies like life itself
Off to the right in Kansas? She goes toward   the blazing-bare lake
Her skirts neat   her hands and face warmed more and more by the air
Rising from pastures of beans   and under her   under chenille
     bedspreads
The farm girls are feeling the goddess in them struggle and rise
     brooding
On the scratch-shining posts of the bed   dreaming of female signs
Of the moon   male blood like iron   of what is really said by the moan
Of airliners passing over them at dead of midwest midnight   passing
Over brush fires   burning out in silence on little hills   and will wake
To see the woman they should be   struggling on the rooftree to become
Stars: for her the ground is closer   water is nearer   she passes
It   then banks   turns   her sleeves fluttering differently as she rolls
Out to face the east, where the sun shall come up from wheatfields
     she must
Do something with water   fly to it   fall in it   drink it   rise
From it   but there is none left upon earth   the clouds have drunk
     it back
The plants have sucked it down   there are standing toward her only
The common fields of death   she comes back from flying to falling
Returns to a powerful cry   the silent scream with which she blew down
The coupled door of the airliner   nearly   nearly losing hold
Of what she has done   remembers   remembers the shape at the heart
Of cloud   fashionably swirling   remembers she still has time to die
Beyond explanation. Let her now take off her hat in summer air the
     contour

Of cornfields   and have enough time to kick off her one remaining
Shoe with the toes   of the other foot   to unhook her stockings
With calm fingers, noting how fatally easy it is to undress in midair
Near death   when the body will assume without effort any position
Except the one that will sustain it   enable it to rise   live
Not die   nine farms hover close   widen   eight of them separate,
     leaving
One in the middle   then the fields of that farm do the same   there
     is no
Way to back off   from her chosen ground   but she sheds the jacket
With its silver sad impotent wings   sheds the bat's guiding tailpiece
Of her skirt   the lightning-charged clinging of her blouse   the
     intimate
Inner flying-garment of her slip in which she rides like the holy ghost
Of a virgin   sheds the long windsocks of her stockings   absurd
Brassiere   then feels the girdle required by regulations squirming
Off her: no longer monobuttocked   she feels the girdle flutter   shake
In her hand   and float   upward   her clothes rising off her
     ascending
Into cloud   and fights away from her head the last sharp dangerous
     shoe
Like a dumb bird   and now will drop in   SOON   now will drop

In like this   the greatest thing that ever came to Kansas   down
     from all
Heights   all levels of American breath   layered in the lungs
     from the frail
Chill of space to the loam where extinction slumbers in corn tassels
     thickly
And breathes like rich farmers counting: will come among them after
Her last superhuman act   the last slow careful passing of her hands
All over her unharmed body   desired by every sleeper in his dream:
Boys finding for the first time their loins filled with heart's blood
Widowed farmers whose hands float under light covers to find
     themselves
Arisen at sunrise   the splendid position of blood unearthly drawn
Toward clouds   all feel something   pass over them as she passes
Her palms over *her* long legs   *her* small breasts   and deeply between
Her thighs   her hair shot loose from all pins   streaming in the wind
Of her body   let her come openly   trying at the last second to land

Falling 2 9 7

On her back   This is it   THIS
                                        All those who find her impressed
In the soft loam   gone down   driven well into the image of her body
The furrows for miles flowing in upon her where she lies very deep
In her mortal outline   in the earth as it is in cloud   can tell nothing
But that she is there   inexplicable   unquestionable   and remember
That something broke in them as well   and began to live and die more
When they walked for no reason into their fields to where the whole
     earth
Caught her   interrupted her maiden flight   told her how to lie
     she cannot
Turn   go away   cannot move   cannot slide off it and assume another
Position   no sky-diver with any grin could save her   hold her in
     his arms
Plummet with her   unfold above her his wedding silks   she can no
     longer
Mark the rain with whirling women that take the place of a dead wife
Or the goddess in Norwegian farm girls   or all the back-breaking
     whores
Of Wichita. All the known air above her is not giving up quite one
Breath   it is all gone   and yet not dead   not anywhere else
Quite   lying still in the field on her back   sensing the smells
Of incessant growth try to lift her   a little sight left in the corner
Of one eye   fading   seeing something wave   lies believing
That she could have made it   at the best part of her brief goddess
State   to water   gone in headfirst   come out smiling   invulnerable
Girl in a bathing-suit ad   but she is lying like a sunbather at the last
Of moonlight   half-buried in her impact on the earth   not far
From a railroad trestle   a water tank   she could see if she could
Raise her head from her modest hole   with her clothes beginning
To come down all over Kansas   into bushes   on the dewy sixth green
Of a golf course   one shoe   her girdle coming down fantastically
On a clothesline, where it belongs   her blouse on a lightning rod:

Lies in the fields   in *this* field   on her broken back as though on
A cloud she cannot drop through   while farmers sleepwalk without
Their women from houses   a walk like falling toward the far waters
Of life   in moonlight   toward the dreamed eternal meaning of
     their farms
Toward the flowering of the harvest in their hands   that tragic cost

298

Feels herself go   go toward   go outward   breathes at last fully
Not   and tries   less   once   tries   tries   AH, GOD—